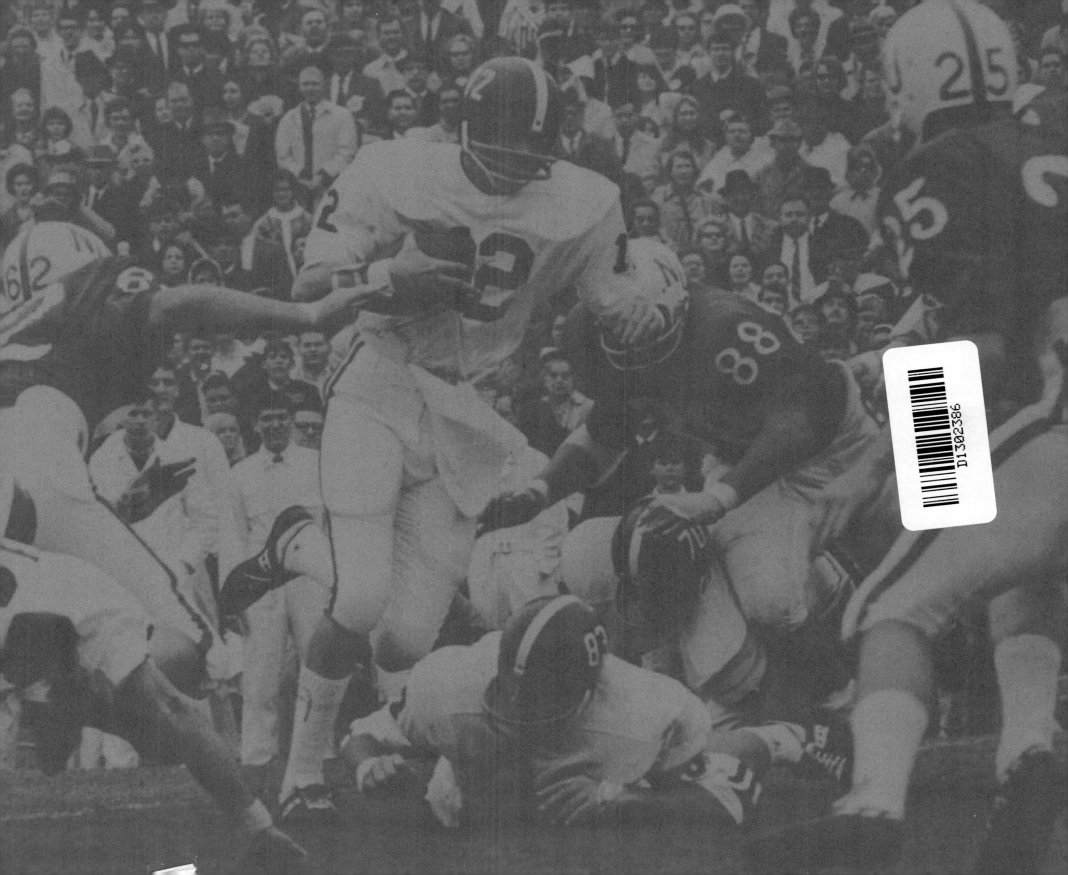

# UNIVERSITY FOOTBALL
# ALABAMA

# UNIVERSITY FOOTBALL
# ALABAMA

## JACK CLARY

Published by World Publications Group, Inc.
140 Laurel Street
East Bridgewater, MA 02333
www.wrldpub.net

ISBN 1-57215-038-6
978-1-57215-038-6

Printed and bound in China by SNP Leefung Printers Limited.

1 2 3 4 5   06 05 03 02

**Previous pages: An
indomitable spirit (page
1), a swarming defense
(page 2), and diehard
fans who follow the team
everywhere (page 3) have
always been the hallmarks
of Alabama football.**

**These pages: Alabama's
football history includes
more bowl appearances
than any other team.
Here the 1937 team
prepares for the Rose
Bowl against California.**

# CONTENTS

Preface....................................................6

1.  Tide Football Is Born............................10

2.  The Magnificent Wade Era...................20

3.  The Frank Thomas Era.........................30

4.  The Tide Struggles...............................40

5.  The Bear is Back and So is 'Bama..........48

6.  'Bama Beat Rolls On.............................64

7.  In the Bear's Image..............................74

8.  A Rollercoaster Era..............................86

9.  Hectic Times.......................................98

10. The Tide vs. The Tiger........................110

11. Bowlin' With 'Bama............................124

Alabama Crimson Tide Football Records......140

Index and Photo Credits.......................142

# PREFACE

**O**ver the years, football at the Capstone has amassed an impressive record of achievements. Alabama has won a dozen national championships and 21 Southeastern Conference titles. They are one of just seven teams in NCAA history to win more than 100 games in a decade (1970s) with a record of 103-16-1. That included seven Southeastern Conference titles and three national championships. Alabama is fifth on the all-time victory list among all Division I teams. Paul (Bear) Bryant finished his coaching career in 1982 as college football's all-time leader in victories with 316 (a record that has since been replaced); and still leads all SEC coaches with 13 conference titles a quarter century after coaching his last team. Alabama has played in more games, and has had more victories and championships than any team in SEC history. They've had more 10-victory seasons than any other Division I school. Alabama is the only SEC team to win a conference championship in every decade since the conference was formed in the thirties. They're No. 1 in terms of bowl games and bowl victories. Alabama has some 20 former players and coaches enshrined in the College Football Hall of Fame.

It is not beyond exaggeration to say that Alabama football is more than just a game to its adherents. It is a way of life—why else would more than 92,000 fans show up for its annual spring scrimmage in 2007, forcing school officials to turn away thousands more because Bryant-Denny Stadium and its surrounding area

**Right: Alabama's famed "Red elephant" mascot has been a symbol of its success since 1930.**

**Opposite left: Crimson Tide fever was so white hot after Nick Saban was named the new head coach in 2007 that a record 92,000 fans turned out for the annual spring game and authorities finally closed access routes to Bryant-Denny Stadium to help maintain crowd control.**

**Opposite right: Beating archrival Auburn is the ultimate triumph every season, and a reward often is an impromptu shower like the one coach Gene Stallings got after the Tide defeated the Tigers 16-7 in 1990.**

simply could not accommodate any more spectators. And this was in the end of April, no less.

When Alabama football is mentioned thoughts immediately turn to one man: Paul (Bear) Bryant. Bryant played for the Tide in the mid-thirties as the "other" end opposite college and pro football Hall of Famer Don Hutson. While Hutson went on to become one of the greatest pass receivers in National Football League history, Bryant turned to coaching and quickly established himself after serving as an instructor in the Navy's V-5 pilot training program during World War II. He became head coach at the University of Kentucky in 1946 and compiled a record of 60-23-5 over the next eight seasons before leaving to revitalize a downtrodden program at Texas A&M University.

Saying "mother has called me," Bryant returned to Alabama as head coach in 1958, again confronting a downtrodden football program, which had won only eight games in the previous four seasons. He never had a losing season during his quarter century as the Tide's head coach. In his second year at Alabama—and for every year thereafter until he finished coaching in 1982—his teams played

in a bowl game as part of college football's post-season celebration, sometimes playing for the national championship when Alabama football was synonymous with the best the sport had to offer.

That is how Alabama football is perceived. While Bryant is the most prominent factor in that great tradition, the ascent to greatness really had it roots early in the twentieth century when Dr. George (Mike) Denny became the university's president. Not only was Denny a great administrator and a firm adherent of college football's importance as a rallying point for students and alumni alike, but he established the conviction that his school's reputation and income were in direct proportion to its success on the playing field.

A decade later, Wallace Wade brought maturity to its football culture as the first of a line of great coaches who lifted Alabama toward the heights of college football's world. This was further strengthened when Frank Thomas succeeded him in 1931 as head coach for the next 15 seasons. These two men created golden eras of football at Alabama, and it was that tradition that Bryant revived and nurtured during his quarter century at the Capstone.

Much of that tradition centered around winning and those who were so instrumental in that regard included some of the greatest players

in college football history: Johnny Mack Brown, later a fabled star of Hollywood's western movie scene; Millard (Dixie) Howell; Don Hutson; linemen such as Fred Sington; Frank Howard, who later won 160 games in 30 seasons as head coach at Clemson; Pooley Hubert; Bill Lee; Don Whitmire, who also starred at the Naval Academy during World War II and later became a distinguished admiral in the Navy; Vaughan Mancha, Billy Neighbors, and John Hannah; receivers Ozzie Newsome, David Bailey, Ray Perkins, Freddie Milons; quarterbacks Joe Namath, Ken Stabler, Steve Sloan, Pat Trammell, Mike Shula; kickers Van Tiffin, Michael Proctor; running backs Riley Smith, Johnny Cain, Harry Gilmer, Bobby Marlow, Ed Salem, Johnny Musso, Bobby Humphrey, Sherman Williams, Shaun Alexander; and defensive players Hootie Ingram, Leroy Jordan, Cornelius Bennett, Derrick Thomas, John Mangum, Deshea Townsend.

Alabama built its football program long ago on the premise that a school can be successful in the classrooms and laboratories and still be successful on the gridiron. You don't even have to be an Alabama fan to acknowledge that this mission has been accomplished, and for that reason above all else, the Crimson Tide has earned its niche as one of college football's greatest success stories.

Opposite left: Wallace Wade brought Alabama its first national recognition during his eight-season tenure from 1923 to 1930.

Opposite right: Coach Frank Thomas turned out three unbeaten teams and two national champions, including his 1934 team, from 1931 to 1946.

Above: Paul (Bear) Bryant and Alabama football are forever linked because he won 232 games and six national championships in 25 seasons.

Left: Ray Perkins (catching ball) was a fine end at Alabama under Bear Bryant, and then succeeded him as head coach in 1983.

# 1
# TIDE FOOTBALL IS BORN

W. B. BANKHEAD

As strange as it may sound, particularly to hundreds of thousands of staunch University of Alabama football fans, the great and nationally-renowned football program that they worship year-after-year had its roots early in the last decade of the nineteenth century on the bucolic campus of Phillips-Exeter Academy some 1000 miles away in Andover, Massachusetts.

Stranger still, it took a death in the family of a curly-haired, stocky native of Livingston, Alabama, named William G. Little ("W.G." to his friends) to bring about its birth at the Capstone. Little had gone to Phillips-Exeter in 1891 to prepare himself to enter Yale University the following year, but a family death ended those plans when he was forced to return home.

During his brief time at Phillips-Exeter, Little discovered the sport of football, whose rules and playing style had recently been revised by Yale coach Walter Camp to combine the best of rugby and soccer with the variations that had been developed since the sport had first been played on a college level in 1869. This new style had caught on at eastern colleges and prep schools and now was spreading its roots across the country.

Little enrolled at the University of Alabama, then a school in Tuscaloosa made up of about 500 male students whose athletic pursuits were pretty much limited to baseball, gymnastics, and track. His passion for football had not abated after leaving Phillips-Exeter, and as he spread his message among his new schoolmates, he even hauled out his old uniform and a football to illustrate his points. Their curiosity soon turned to rabid enthusiasm and they eagerly accepted his suggestion to form a team.

The University agreed and so was born Alabama's great football heritage with Little, forever known as "father of Alabama football," as captain of the 17-man squad; soon thereafter, Eugene Beaumont was named the first head coach. Like Little, Beaumont had cut his football teeth in the east at the University of Pennsylvania.

Opposite: Alabama's first
football team in 1892
included William Bankhead,
later the speaker of the U.S.
House of Representatives
and father of famed actress
Tallulah Bankhead.

Left: Yale's loss became
Alabama football's biggest
gain when William G.
Little decided to return to
his home state instead of
attending the Ivy League
school, enrolling at the
Capstone and putting
together the first team and
thus becoming the "father of
Alabama football."

**Right: Alabama's first team poses for a group photo in 1892. Eugene Beaumont (top row, with hat) was hired as head coach because he had played the sport at the University of Pennsylvania.**

All of this had transpired in the early fall of 1892, so it wasn't until November 11, at Lakeview Park in Birmingham, that Alabama played its first game. Actually, this was to be a warm-up scrimmage against a team of high school players before the team played the Birmingham Athletic Club the next day. But official school records still list it as the first game and a 56-0 victory. The following day, however, Alabama suffered its first loss, 5-4, when the A.C.'s J.P. Ross kicked a 63-yard field goal in the final minute. Little had scored the Tide's only touchdown earlier in the game, but the extra point was somehow missed and that was the final difference (field goals counted five points and touchdowns only four back then).

The teams had a rematch four weeks later, and the Tide won 14-0, keyed by D.A. Grayson's 65-yard touchdown run. The team then finished its first season on February 22, 1893, by losing to intrastate rival Auburn 32-22 while also starting one of college football's most colorful rivalries. Still undecided after more than a century was whether that game was Alabama's final contest of the 1892 season, or the first game of the 1893 season.

What followed over the next few years was a series of firsts—some good, some not so good, as in the aftermath of a ruling by the school's board of directors that the team could not play off campus. The program nosedived, helped also by the brutal physical nature of the game at that time with its massed formations that injuries abounded. Things got so bad the school suspended the sport for the 1897 season.

In 1904, the first season Alabama played ten games, it defeated Georgia 36-0, giving the program an overall record of 32-21. In the century-plus since that milestone, the Tide's overall win-loss record has never been under .500, and for years, it has been ranked among the top ten winningest college programs.

Yet, it wasn't until 1906 when J.W.H. (Doc) Pollard was hired and became the first coach to win 20 games (20-4-5 from 1906–09) that the football program stabilized. The star of his teams was running back Derrill Pratt who, in 1907, played in the first game he ever saw and did so after just three days of practice. He later became the first Alabama graduate to play in baseball as an outfielder for the New York Yankees.

Still, it was another six years after Pollard left in 1915 that the Tide finally produced its first All-America player, W.T. (Bully) Vandegraaff. The last of three brothers to play for Alabama—and all were four-year starters—he weighed less than 150 pounds but still played tackle and fullback; scored at least one

**Right: Eli Abbott was the star of Alabama's first football teams. He served as the Tide's coach from 1893-95, and again in 1903.**

Left: Riggs Stephenson (left) and Joe Sewell not only starred for Alabama's football team, but later played in the World Series while members of the Cleveland Indians. Stephenson also played for the 1929 Chicago Cubs in a World Series while Joe Sewell was inducted into Baseball's Hall of Fame in 1976.

Above: W. T. (Bully) Vandegraaff was Alabama's first All-America player. He was a running back and lineman from 1912-15, and following graduation he enrolled at West Point and played for Army.

touchdown in every game that he played as a running back; and was the team's kicker whose career punting average was an astounding 55 yards per kick. In his 1915 senior season, he kicked 12 field goals and 26 of 28 extra points. His most memorable game was producing 17 of his team's 23 points during a 23-10 victory over Sewanee, then one of the South's most powerful teams. With the score tied in the fourth quarter, he recovered a fumble and returned it 65 yards for a touchdown, added the extra point, and later kicked two field goals to cement the win.

When Charles Bernier was hired as athletic director as the twenties began, Alabama's football took a giant step forward. A vigorous recruiter of coaching and playing talent, Bernier hired head coach Xen Scott and then recruited future stars like Luke and Joe Sewell and Riggs Stephenson. All three players later had outstanding major league baseball careers, Luke as a pennant-winning manager of the 1944 St. Louis Browns and Joe as a 1976 inductee in the Hall of Fame who had played in two World Series with the Chicago Cubs and Cleveland Indians.

Scott, along with assistant coach Hank Crisp who coached at Alabama for 30 years under five coaches and also had two tours as athletic director, brought much-needed stability to the football program and really paved the way for the Tide's great success after he left in 1922. His 1919 team won eight of nine games and his 1920 team was the first to win 10 games with its 10-1 record. That team even played three games in one week, starting with the season's only loss to Georgia. Four days later, Alabama beat Mississippi State 24-7 as Stephenson completed 10 passes and three days after that, the Tide went to Cleveland, Ohio, and defeated Case College 40-0 as Stephenson and Al Clemens each scored two touchdowns.

But the gem among Scott's 29 victories was a stunning 9-7 upset victory in 1922 over the University of Pennsylvania before 25,000 people in Philadelphia. Few gave the Tide a chance to win, but after trailing 7-3 for most of the game, Bill Bay's 35-yard run and Shorty Probst's recovery of Pooley Hubert's fumble at the Penn goal line produced the winning points, in a 9-7 victory. This game became the turning point for Alabama football because it proved then, and soon established for all time, that the Tide could win against any team in the country.

**Left: One of Alabama's most significant victories during the first part of the 20th century was a rollicking 23-10 win over Sewanee, then one of the region's most powerful teams. W.T (Bully) Vandegraaff accounted for 17 of the Tide's points, including a touchdown after he knocked the ball from the hands of Sewanee's passer, caught it in mid-air, and ran 65 yards for the score.**

**Right:** Xen Scott's most significant victory in his four seasons was a 9-7 win in Philadelphia over the University of Pennsylvania in 1922.

**Center:** This archival photo shows Alabama's players and coaches being greeted by a crowd of adoring fans at the Tuscaloosa railroad depot when the team returned home in 1922 after a stunning 9-7 victory over the University of Pennsylvania. Most experts had declared the game would be a "breather" for the Quakers, but the Tide came from behind in the fourth quarter when Shorty Probst pounced on teammate Pooley Hubert's fumble in the end zone for a touchdown.

**Far right:** A young Ronald Reagan (left), then a Hollywood movie star, chats with legendary Alabama athletic coach Hank Crisp. Crisp, though he had lost his right hand in a farm accident at age 13, was Alabama's football line coach for 30 years under five different coaches, spent 18 years as head basketball coach, and coached track and baseball. He also served two tours as athletic director.

# 2

# THE MAGNIFICENT WADE ERA

One of the most significant advances made by Alabama's football program in its early years occurred in 1912 when Dr. George (Mike) Denny became the university's president. He firmly believed that intercollegiate football was a rallying point for students and alumni, and that the success of his football program would produce dual benefits in growing both Alabama's reputation and its income.

"The better the team, the larger the gate, the better the team," was his working rule. He spent many fall afternoons watching the team practice, and he never missed a game. Three stadiums on Alabama's campus have carried his name, including the current 82,000-seat Bryant Denny Stadium that shares his name with legendary coach Paul (Bear) Bryant. (The Tide also claims 83,000-seat Legion Field in Birmingham as its other "home" field.)

But Denny's greatest legacy to Alabama's football program occurred in 1923 when, with more than a bit of luck, he hired Wallace Wade to be his school's head coach. Wade was on the brink of signing a contract with Kentucky but had an offer from Alabama in his hip pocket. Kentucky's athletic committee hemmed and hawed about the final decision while it kept Wade sitting in a hotel lobby. When an hour had passed with no decision, a furious Wade had enough and marched into the meeting room and, in effect, resigned before he ever officially had the job. He also told the committee that he was going to Alabama before it had ever finally agreed to hire him. Moreover, he guaranteed that no Kentucky team ever would beat one of his Alabama teams—and none ever did in the eight games they played against each other. After that declaration, he

called Alabama and said he was ready to lead its football team, and the Tide immediately welcomed him.

Wade had a drill sergeant's manner from his army days fighting in France during World War I. A disciplinarian and a perfectionist, he had a hands-on coaching style that often included getting down on the ground with a player, be he a first- or third-stringer, to demonstrate exactly what he wanted. His teams often practiced a play for two months before using it, and when he spotted mistakes during practice, he'd order countless repetitions until he was satisfied with the execution.

His eight-season run (1923-1930) boosted the Tide into the elite category among the nation's college football teams with a record of 61 victories, 13 losses, and three ties. Alabama won three national championships during its unbeaten seasons of 1925-26, and 1930; made three Rose Bowl appearances, defeating Washington and Washington State and tying Stanford; and compiled a school record unbeaten streak of 24 games, from the final game of 1924 through the third game of the 1927 season. The record lasted for more than a half century, until Bryant's 1978-80 teams produced 28 consecutive wins.

The team's rosters during that time were dotted with some of Alabama's greatest players—Hall of Famers Johnny Mack Brown; lineman Frank Howard, who also became a Hall of Fame coach after a 30-season career at Clemson; quarterback Pooley Hubert, Alabama's second All-America player whose 1922-25 teams compiled a 31-6-2 record; and tackle Fred Sington, whom Notre Dame coach Knute Rockne once called

**Opposite: Wallace Wade's coaching genius put Alabama among the nation's top college teams during his 1923-30 tenure. His teams won 61 games, including 20 in a row, and had two victories and a tie in three Rose Bowl appearances.**

"the greatest tackle in football history." Wade, who also had a distinguished 16-year coaching career at Duke where he won 116 games, was inducted into the Hall of Fame in 1955.

Herschel Caldwell, Bill Buckler, and Hoyt Winslett were other players who starred during the Wade era, but Brown was the team's gem. Nicknamed the "Dothan Antelope" (he was from Dothan, Alabama) because his open-field running style reminded many of an antelope on the move, he was one of four brothers to play for Alabama and the centerpiece of the 1923-25 teams.

**Above: Johnny Mack Brown led a 20-point, seven-minute third quarter explosion against Washington that sent Alabama to a 20-19 victory in its first Rose Bowl appearance in 1926.**

**Right: Johnny Mack Brown was one of Hollywood's first great western movie stars, but from 1923-25 he was unsurpassed as a runner and pass receiver. He was Alabama's greatest all-around player to that time, and one of its best ever.**

**Opposite: Johnny Mack Brown finished his career at Alabama after the 1925 season, but the family tradition carried on as his brother Red Brown carried the ball against Stanford during a 7-7 tie in the 1927 Rose Bowl that capped a second straight national championship and an unbeaten season.**

Brown weighed 180 pounds, a good size for running backs at that time, and he was one of the fastest backs in college football, which made him a fearsome weapon running in the open field. His pass-catching ability gave the Tide another great weapon at a time when backs were rarely featured in a team's pass offense. To enhance his speed, Wade even devised the first pair of "low-cut" football shoes, in a time when everyone wore high tops.

It was after he left Alabama that Brown, who had been active in Alabama's theater program as a student, gained his greatest notoriety when motion pictures with sound transformed Hollywood's movie industry. His career spanned some 200 films, starting with a bit part in the movie *Bugle Call,* and followed soon thereafter with his first starring role opposite famed actress Mary Pickford. In the early thirties, he was acclaimed for his starring role in *Billy the Kid,* and from that time until his retirement in 1952, he was one of America's preeminent western movie stars.

Opposite: Hoyt (Wu) Winslett (in dark jersey) was one of the star backs on Alabama's 1925 and 1926 national champion teams.

Above: Winslett was one of the keys to Alabama's back-to-back unbeaten seasons in 1925 and 1926, which culminated with a pair of Rose Bowl appearances. In the 1927 game, the Tide played a 7-7 tie against Pop Warner's great Stanford team.

Left: Running back Johnny Mack Brown triggered a 20-point explosion during a seven-minute span in the third quarter of the 1926 Rose Bowl against the University of Washington, which brought Alabama a 20-19 victory.

**Above:** Fred Sington was a two-time All-America tackle in 1929-30 and is considered one of the greatest linemen in Alabama football history.

**Left:** Halfback "Monk" Campbell (seen here) teamed with John (Sugar) Cain to lead Alabama to a 10-0 record, a national championship, and a Rose Bowl victory in 1930.

**Left: Movie star Marion Davies was "mascot" for both Alabama and Stanford at the 1927 Rose Bowl. Alabama's Emile Barnes is at right.**

At Alabama, Brown always has been revered for his offensive exploits to the point where his defensive skills often were overlooked. Along with linemen Bruce Jones and Buckler, he was one of the keys to the 1924 team holding seven of nine opponents scoreless, including the first six. That team won Alabama's first Southern Conference title (at the time, that conference encompassed every Southern team) and set the stage for its unbeaten seasons in 1925 and 1926.

Wade always maintained the 1925 team had the perfect combination of playing experience, great blocking ability, strong defense, and a varied offense that equally utilized running, passing, and kicking. "It earned its national championship recognition because it mastered a tough schedule, was a high point-scorer, and gave up just one touchdown," he later said. "It also made one of the great comebacks in Rose Bowl history, scoring three touchdowns in six minutes early in the second half to defeat Washington 19-18."

A great deal of Alabama's success in 1925 came when Wade paired Brown and Hubert as the principle backfield combination in his single wing offense. Brown played wingback and tailback, where his running and pass-catching abilities were showcased. Hubert, who had come to Alabama as a tackle, was switched to fullback, and since he was a better passer than Brown, he also handled most of the pass offense. Hubert played linebacker on defense and was a veritable tackling machine. It was said that he made 25 tackles against Georgia Tech and repeated that feat in the Rose Bowl victory over Washington. He, not Brown, was chosen the most valuable player in the Southern Conference as a prelude to the Helms Athletic Foundation and Football Annual both awarding the Tide its first national championship. The following year, Brown and the other fine backs of the 1925 team had graduated, but Wade's team erased any doubts about its worth by shutting out six of its ten opponents and winning another national championship. Only a 7-7 tie against Pop Warner's great Stanford team in a second straight Rose Bowl cost it another perfect season.

The following three seasons brought continued success but not enough for a bowl bid or a conference title, and Tide fans began to grumble. Wade became so irked that he announced before the 1930 season, when his contract would expire, that he was leaving the Capstone.

He did it in unforgettable fashion, with a third undefeated season, a third national championship, and a second Rose Bowl victory. Led by Sington, Howard, and backs John (Sugar)

Cain and "Monk" Campbell, the Tide was rarely pushed to win any of its games. Its biggest victory was 13-0 over Georgia in the final game of the season with a Rose Bowl invite going to the winner.

Wade took 35 players to Pasadena for the Rose Bowl, got all of them into the game, and then enjoyed a ride atop their shoulders after a 24-0 victory over Washington State that ended the first great chapter in Alabama football history.

**Above: Johnny Mack Brown wasn't the only member of his family to play at Alabama. His brother William (right) was also a member of the Tide's 1925 national championship team.**

**Right: "Monk" Campbell carries the ball against Washington State in the 1931 Rose Bowl, during which he scored twice on runs of one and 43 yards and kicked three PATs in the Tide's 24-0 victory.**

# 3

# THE FRANK THOMAS ERA

The genius of Alabama president Dr. George S. (Mike) Denny struck a second time in 1931 when he appointed Frank Thomas as head football coach to succeed Wallace Wade. Thus began a 15-year football era at the Capstone that was even greater than the one that had just concluded under Wade.

Actually, Thomas's appointment had come before Wade's final season in 1930. Alabama fans had become spoiled by their team's two national championships and a Rose Bowl appearance in 1925 and 1926, and forging winning records as Wade

did the next three years apparently wasn't enough to satisfy them. He gradually became disgusted with the criticism and carping during those three successful seasons to the point that, as noted earlier, Wade had agreed to fulfill the final year on his contract in 1930 before leaving to become head coach at Duke.

Wade personally recommended to Denny that Thomas, then one of his assistant coaches, should succeed him in 1931, fully realizing that he was putting him on the spot because Denny demanded only success. "It is my conviction that material is 90 percent, coaching ability is 10 percent," Denny told Thomas after he agreed to take the job. "You will be provided with the 90 percent and you will be held to strict

Opposite: President Herbert Hoover (center, standing, holding hat) poses with the 1931 Alabama team during its post-season visit to Washington, where it played a three-way exhibition game against Georgetown, George Washington, and Catholic universities.

Left: Frank Thomas played for Knute Rockne at Notre Dame and carried The Rock's system to The Capstone, where his meticulous planning and teaching helped to win 115 games, 91 of them coming in a 13-season span from 1933-45.

Right: With the help of a lead block by Millard (Dixie) Howell (57), John (Sugar) Cain starts a 72 yard touchdown run for Alabama's only score in a 6-0 victory over St. Mary's University in California in the final game of the 1932 season.

Left: Coach Frank Thomas and one of his prize pupils, tackle Bill Lee, who was captain of the Tide's unbeaten 1934 national championship team that shut out five opponents and then beat Stanford's famed "Vow Boys" in the Rose Bowl.

accounting for the remaining 10 percent." To add to the pressure, Wade then produced an unbeaten season in 1930 as well as a Rose Bowl victory and the national championship in his final season.

No one could have handled the heat better than Thomas. For the next 15 seasons, from 1931 until illness forced him to resign after the 1946 season, his teams won 115 games, lost 24, and tied seven. Until the season before he stepped down, his 108-20-7 record was unsurpassed in college football. During his tenure, Alabama won two national championships; had four unbeaten seasons; won three Southeast Conference titles and shared a fourth; won four of six bowl games at a time when playing in the post-season was restricted to fewer than a dozen teams each year; had three 14-game winning streaks and another of 13 games; and produced 16 All-America players, including three of its best players ever: running backs Millard (Dixie) Howell and Harry Gilmer and end Don Hutson.

When the College Football Hall of Fame was established in 1951, Thomas was a member of its first group of coaches that included Amos Alonzo Stagg, Glenn (Pop) Warner, and his college coach Knute Rockne, for whom he had played at Notre Dame in 1921-22. After graduation, Thomas turned down an offer to work for his old coach, preferring instead to forge his own record and reputation coaching at the Universities of Georgia and Chattanooga before going to Alabama.

Thomas was a smallish man, at five feet, eight inches and about 160 pounds, but he was a firebrand who feared no one. His first act

**Left: Alabama's 1934 national champions (from left): Linemen Bear Bryant, Bill Lee, Bob Morrow, Kavanaugh Francis, Charlie Marr, Jim Wahtley and Don Hutson; backs Jim Angelich, Joe Demyanovich, Riley Smith, and Dixie Howell.**

**Above: Halfback Dixie Howell ran, passed, kicked, and played defense better than anyone in Alabama history from 1932-34.**

as head coach was to junk Wade's single-wing offense and install the Notre Dame system that he had learned under Rockne. He used it throughout his 15 seasons at Alabama, even after the T-formation had taken over as the sport's favorite offense.

Thomas inherited few experienced players because of graduation, but after two seasons, he had a 17-3 record. Despite the winning record, Alabama fans started grumbling again. There were no bowl games, except the Rose Bowl, to mollify the fans of successful teams, and, incredibly, in 1933, his job had become tenuous. But proving that coaching acumen is sometimes a late starter, he had a pair of saviors in Howell and Hutson. First ticketed to be only the team's punter in 1933, Howell became the starting running back after showcasing his great talent in mop-up action in the season's opening game. When he finished his career in 1934, he had become a legend. Some still claim he was the greatest all-around player in Alabama history and the Tide's record book still rings with his achievements, which included 1,508 career rushing yards and a gaudy 6.3 yards-per-rush average. In 1933, he totaled 1,437 yards and had another 1,157 in 1934.

Like all great players, he saved his best for last—the final game of the 1934 season against Vanderbilt with a Rose Bowl bid at stake. He rushed for 162 yards, added another 124 from punt returns, and had a 40-yard punting average. It all added up to a 34-0 victory. Their win over Stanford in the Rose Bowl is covered later in the book.

Howell was the centerpiece of a great offensive trio with ends Don Hutson and Paul

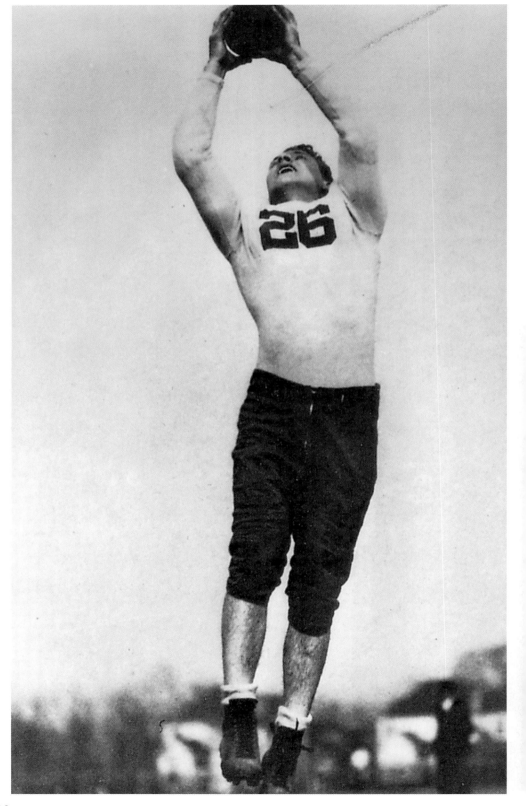

**Above: Riley Smith was quarterback of the Tide's 1934 national championship team.**

**Right: End Don Hutson was the star receiver for Alabama's 1934 national champions, but his greatest fame came in the NFL with the Green Bay Packers.**

(Bear) Bryant that helped to produce two SEC titles, a national championship, and a Rose Bowl victory. Hutson and Bryant both were natives of Arkansas. Hutson had come to Alabama to play baseball and joined the football team only because he missed athletic competition in the fall. He became an incomparable pass receiver, and his great speed made him a fearsome weapon as a receiver and defensive back.

Bryant, who later became Alabama's most renowned head coach, always was referred to as the "other end." Despite his ability to run a 10-second hundred-yard dash, blocking was his greatest asset. Along with fullback Joe Demyanovich, quarterback Riley Smith, halfback Jim Angelich, and lineman Bill Lee, Howell, Hutson, and Bryant helped Alabama

**Left: Tailback Joe Kilgrow was a star for Frank Thomas, leading Alabama to a perfect season in 1936, two SEC titles in 1936-37, and a trip to the 1938 Rose Bowl.**

**Below: Kilgrow (dark jersey, with ball) sets up the game-winning field goal in a 9-7 victory over Vanderbilt that clinched a trip to the 1938 Rose Bowl.**

compile a 17-1-1 record in 1933-34 and win the 1934 national championship after an unbeaten season that included a 29-13 Rose Bowl victory over Stanford.

Two years later, in 1936, the Tide was unbeaten with only a scoreless tie to blemish its record, but was ignored by the bowls. That snub became the impetus for Thomas to drive his 1937 team to a second straight unbeaten season in which it won all nine games, helped by a defense that allowed just 20 points and shut out six opponents. When it uncharacteristically committed eight turnovers against California in the 1938 Rose Bowl, the Tide lost 13-0.

Alabama didn't reach national championship status again until 1941, once again quieting its grumbling fans with a 9-2 record that included a 29-21 victory in the Cotton Bowl against Texas A&M; and Thomas repeated his team's bowl feat the following year when he brought an equally talented team, led by running back Bobby Jack Jenkins and tackle Don Whitmire, to the Orange Bowl where it defeated Boston College 37-21 to cap an 8-3 season.

World War II intervened, and Alabama suspended its football program for the 1943 season after losing stars like Jenkins and Whitmire to the Naval Academy. But with a team dubbed "Thomas's War Babies" because it was made up primarily of freshmen and 4-F students who either were ineligible for military service or awaited a call-up, he regrouped in 1944 with a team good enough to post a 5-1-2 record and barely lose in the final minutes to Duke, 29-26, in the Sugar Bowl.

The Tide's 1945 team compiled a perfect record and went to the Rose Bowl, where it upset Southern California 34-14 with a team that Thomas considered his finest ever at Alabama. His defense was top-ranked in the nation, and the offense was ranked No. 2 as it outscored opponents by an average score of 43-8. The team's star, as he had been in 1944, was Gilmer, a 160-pound triple-threat back who became one of the finest passers in college football history. "I never saw anyone who knew so well what to do under all conditions," Thomas said of

**Right: Harry Gilmer rivaled Dixie Howell as Alabama's most prolific offensive player.**

**Center: Bobby Jenkins goes up and over against Boston College during Alabama's 37-21 come-from-behind win in the 1943 Orange Bowl. Jenkins scored twice in Alabama's first trip to that post-season game.**

**Far right: Gilmer (No. 52) on one of 11 carries that netted him 116 yards and a TD in the Tide's 34-14 win over Southern California in the 1946 Rose Bowl.**

Gilmer. "I never recall him throwing a bad or wild pass." Gilmer completed nearly 69 percent of his passes that year, including 26 for touchdowns, and his rushing produced 1,457 yards, or nearly ten yards per carry.

All of this success had exacted such a fearsome toll on Thomas that in 1946 he really was a part-time coach because of his frail health. The team won seven of its 11 games but Thomas resigned when the season ended and continued as athletic director until 1951. He passed away in 1954 at the relatively young age of 56, leaving a legacy that has been matched only by one of his pupils, Bear Bryant.

# 4

# THE TIDE STRUGGLES

ome have declared that the law of averages finally caught up to Alabama football during the dozen years after the end of World War II. The halcyon days enjoyed by Tide fans during a glorious quarter-century under Wallace Wade and Frank Thomas faded to pleasant memories as Alabama's rivals finally caught up and matched their excellence. Some claimed that the successors to Wade and Thomas, Harold (Red) Drew and J.B. Whitworth, could not match the coaching ability of their two predecessors.

Whatever it was—and it was really a combination of all three elements—the Crimson Tide came back to the pack after World War II when the team compiled a record of 58 victories, 52 losses, and 9 ties from 1947-56. Actually, the program under Drew turned in a respectable record (by most standards, though not what Tide fans had been used to) of 54-28-7 from 1947-54; then it slipped badly under Whitworth to just 4-24-2 in the next three years.

There was no indication that Alabama's football fortunes would begin to dip during Drew's tenure. He came to Alabama after finishing his first season as head coach at Mississippi in 1946, where his team had won just two of nine games. But he had been end coach at Alabama under Thomas for 11 years

**Right: Alabama tacklers get after a Mississippi State running back during the Tide's 42-19 victory. Alabama finished that season with a 9-2 record and a trip to the Orange Bowl where the Tide soundly defeated Syracuse.**

**Opposite: Harold (Red) Drew succeeded Frank Thomas as Alabama's head coach after ill health forced Thomas to give up the job in 1947. Drew had been Thomas's end coach. He had six winning seasons during his eight-year stint and brought the Tide to three bowl games.**

before that and was Thomas's personal choice as a successor. Drew inherited the famed "War Babies," led by All-America running back Harry Gilmer, who had helped revitalize Alabama's football program in 1944 and were then seniors. That group had a great senior season, helping the Tide to an 8-2 regular season record. Unfortunately, their final game at Alabama, against Texas and its great star Bobby Layne in the Sugar Bowl, was a disappointing 28-7 loss. Gilmer had the worst day of his career, completing just three of 11 passes and gaining only five rushing yards.

Alabama got off to a pair of slow (1-2-1) starts during the 1948-49 seasons but still recovered with late-season surges to compile winning records. During this time, a fractured relationship with intra-state rival Auburn was repaired by legislative mandate, and the teams played each other for the first time in 41 years in 1948. Alabama made up for lost time and won the game by a whopping score of 55-0; Auburn soon settled down and won the next game. That historic rivalry is covered in a separate chapter elsewhere in the book.

**Left:** In addition to his job as Alabama's quarterback, Bart Starr also was the team's punter during the early 1950s. When he became an all-pro and future Hall of Fame player with the Green Bay Packers, he also retained the job as backup punter.

**Right:** Tackle Jess Richardson (68), and backs Tommy Lewis (42), and Bobby Marlow (32), celebrate Alabama's 61-6 victory over Syracuse in the 1953 Orange Bowl.

**Opposite:** Alabama crushed Syracuse 61-6 in the 1953 Orange Bowl with a 586-yard offensive performance that was keyed by its power-packed backfield of, from left, Bobby Marlow, Tommy Lewis, Clell Hobson, and Bobby Luna. Hobson threw a pair of TD passes, and Luna and Lewis each scored twice.

Alabama fans had longed for another great player in the mold of Johnny Mack Brown, Dixie Howell, and Gilmer. They finally got him in 1950 when Bobby Marlow, a young sophomore from Troy, Alabama, had five games, including the last three of the season, in which he rushed for more than 100 yards. That streak began with 180 against Georgia Tech during a whopping 54-19 victory and continued the following week with 100 against Florida. He then ended the season with 113 against Auburn.

It's been more than half a century since he played for Alabama, but like his performance against Georgia Tech, his feats still adorn Alabama's record book. His average gain of 13.8 yards per carry that day still ranks No. 3 among all Alabama running backs who have rushed more than ten times in a game; his 7.5 yards per rush during the 1950 season still ranks first; his 233 yards against Auburn in 1951 ranks third all-time; his career total of 2,560 rushing yards, compiled in 1950-52 over a 32-game career, is fifth all-time but ranked No. 1 until 1971 when it was broken by Johnny Musso; his 92-yard touchdown run against Georgia Tech in 1950 is third longest in Tide history; and his 26 career rushing touchdowns rank sixth. Ironically, he was the team's top runner in 1951 when Alabama suffered its first losing season (5-6) since 1900. The following season, he had a career high 950 yards, including 174 against Virginia Tech.

**Below: A half dozen Tide players—Charles Malcolm, John McBride, William J. Stone, Bobby Duke, Bobby Luna, Hyrle Ivy—relax during the closing minutes of Alabama's momentous 61-6 Orange Bowl victory over Syracuse in 1953.**

**Right: Fullback Tommy Lewis was a three-season starter for the Tide in 1952-54 and coach Red Drew called him the best fullback he ever coached.**

**Opposite: Bobby Luna was a very versatile and colorful backup running back for Alabama during his four varsity seasons from 1951 thru 1954. He played behind Bobby Marlow and Corky Tharp.**

**Opposite: Tommy Lewis (center, white helmet) scores his second TD in the 1953 Orange Bowl.**

**Left: Hootie Ingram (20), a future Alabama athletic director, breaks up a Syracuse pass.**

Drew produced his best team in 1952, helped by the emergence of sophomore backs Bobby Luna and Corky Tharp. Tharp was so good that Drew promoted him from Marlow's backup to starting left halfback, and he moved Marlow to right halfback. He started Tommy Lewis at fullback and called him the best fullback he ever coached. He also began grooming a young quarterback named Bart Starr, whose greatest days in football lay many years ahead in Green Bay, Wisconsin, where he became an NFL Hall of Fame player for Vince Lombardi.

Alabama took its 9-2 record to the 1953 Orange Bowl and overwhelmed Syracuse, 61-6. At one point in the fourth quarter, an Orange Bowl committeeman approached the game's timekeeper and suggested that he keep the clock running so that the game, then running nearly three hours, would not be cut off from television before its conclusion. Of course, the request was denied but the Tide's offense produced nearly 600 yards of offense after leading by only 7-6 at the end of the first quarter and 20-6 at the half. "I just couldn't stop them," Drew said later about his team's 40-point second half. "We didn't try to run up the score. Everybody just figured we had a particularly good football team on that day."

Marlow was gone in 1953, but Tharp took over the offense during a 6-2-3 season that got Alabama invited to play Rice in the Cotton Bowl. That game, won by Rice, produced one of the most astounding plays in college football history, involving Tommy Lewis and Rice's Dickie Moegle, and it is covered in the chapter on Alabama's bowl history.

Alabama's football fortunes began to nosedive in 1954 with a 4-5-2 record, and Drew was replaced by another former Alabama player, J.B. Whitworth. He had been the kicker on Alabama's 1931 Rose Bowl champions, and at the time of his hiring at Alabama, he had a 22-27-2 record in five years as head coach at Oklahoma State. Whitworth's tenure was disastrous, beginning with an 0-10 season in 1955, and a pair of 2-7-1 years in 1956-57. At one point, Alabama had a 20-game winless streak. Even worse, archrival Auburn had outscored the Tide 100-7 in their three games during that time.

Suddenly, it was panic mode at the Capstone and that called for a radical solution. His name was Paul (Bear) Bryant and he was coming home to Alabama not only to save his school's proud football legacy, but to become one of college football's immortal coaches.

# 5

# THE BEAR IS BACK AND SO IS 'BAMA

"The reason, the only reason, I'm going back is because my school called me."

Thus, did Paul William Bryant, long nicknamed "Bear," tell everyone in late 1957 that he had agreed to become head coach at Alabama. In his mind, he was "going back" to a school where, as a player, he had been an integral part of a storied football program nearly a quarter century earlier, and from which he had ventured to become one of college football's finest coaches.

In reality, as he noted years later, he never wanted, nor ever intended, to return to Alabama. In fact, he had passed up several opportunities in previous years to return but those who wanted him wouldn't accept his refusals. They kept reminding him what the school had done for him, and how he was the only coach who could return it to its former football glory. He didn't really believe those pleas but he started to pay attention to the mail from talented Alabama high school players who vowed they would come and play for him.

"I just couldn't refuse," he said.

He was being asked to perform a labor of love in an atmosphere of despair when he began his Alabama coaching career in the 1958 season. Though he had been a very successful head coach in three

previous jobs at Maryland, Kentucky, and Texas A&M, he obviously had a subliminal love for Alabama that only surfaced after he took the job and saw the joy that his wife, Mary Harmon, had experienced when she arrived in Tuscaloosa. "I wish I had made the move years earlier," he later said.

He also had his own personal feelings about "coming home." Playing football at Alabama had helped to lift him from the raw poverty that had engulfed his early life in Arkansas, and provided the opportunity that he had so badly coveted to forge his own success. He had always treasured the years when he played for Frank Thomas and reveled in the satisfaction that came from being on championship teams with other great players like Bill Lee, Dixie Howell, and Don Hutson, who was also his college roommate and lifelong friend.

Thomas always believed that Bryant had the potential to become a fine head coach because he always seemed a step ahead of everyone else in figuring out how best to succeed on

**Left: Bear Bryant had been head coach at Maryland, Kentucky, and Texas A&M before returning to his alma mater. When he retired after the 1982 season, he had won 325 games, more than any coach in history up to that time.**

**Opposite: Paul (Bear) Bryant, 6′2″ and 196 pounds, was an Arkansas native known as "the other end" on Alabama's 1934 national championship team that featured All-America receiver Don Hutson. He was an assistant coach at his alma mater for several seasons and was named head coach in 1958.**

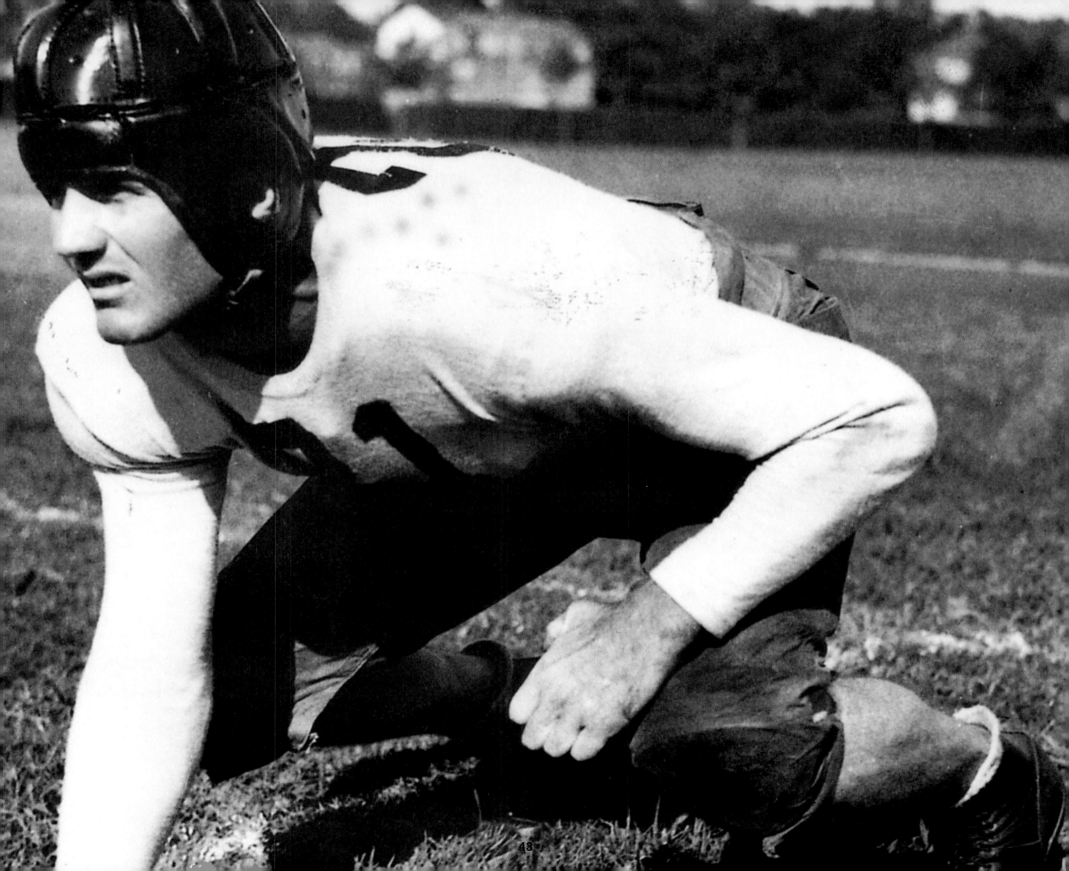

the field. He dissuaded Bryant from following Howell and Hutson into professional football. After Bryant graduated from Alabama in January 1939, Thomas hired him as an assistant coach, the start of what ultimately became a brilliant career.

Bryant's joy in returning to Alabama in 1958 was celebrated equally by the legions of Alabama rooters who had chafed under four straight losing seasons, and five in the seven years since 1951. Most of them didn't know what it meant to lose because the Tide didn't have a losing season from 1900 until 1951 when the team could only manage a 4-5 record. Bryant had been a part of what many of them considered the greatest era of Alabama football when championships and winning seasons came with almost monotonous regularity.

As a young football coach, Bryant made a fine reputation for himself, first at Alabama, then at Vanderbilt under Red Sanders before World War II intervened. Tom Hamilton, who had been an All-America running back at the Naval Academy in the twenties and later its head coach for three years during the thirties, was ordered to develop a massive naval pre-flight training program at several universities around the country to train thousands of aviators the Navy needed for its growing force of aircraft carriers. Part of the curriculum included a vigorous physical training program, including intercollegiate football, and he recruited young college coaches like Bryant to staff it.

**Left: Bear Bryant immediately energized Alabama's offense with a wide open passing game featuring Bobby Skelton passing to players such as end Bill Rice (85).**

**Above: Mike Fracchia's TD helped the Tide defeat Georgia 32-6 in the opener of its 1961 national championship season.**

It became a ladder for success because Bryant, who had coached at both North Carolina and Georgia Pre-Flight, was hired to coach Maryland in 1946 and produced a 6-2-1 record in his only season there. He then moved to Kentucky, where, in eight years, his teams had a 62-23-3 record and went to four bowl games. But that meant his football team had to play second fiddle to Kentucky's famed basketball coach Adolph Rupp, and Bryant soon tired of having to beg for resources.

Texas A&M was desperately seeking a coach and Bryant not only answered the call but immediately created one of college football's great legends. He took two busloads of aspiring but under-performing Aggie players to training camp in Junction, Texas, in the bleak Texas midlands, where he forced them to endure what became a survival program. Those who survived filled just half a bus in returning to school and they won only one game in 1954. But in the next three seasons, they had a 24-4-2 record and won the Southwest Conference championship.

Thus did Alabama get the man who was needed to revitalize its football program. Consider that during his 25 years as Alabama's most famous head coach, Bryant's teams won six national championships; won or shared 13 Southeast Conference titles; never had a losing season; had three perfect seasons; had ten one-loss seasons and six when it lost only twice; compiled the team's longest winning streak ever, 28 games that included the last nine games of the 1978 season through the seventh game of 1980; fashioned other winning streaks of 19, 17, 12, and 11 games; had a post-season record of 13-10-1 in 24 consecutive bowl games, from the Liberty Bowl of 1959 to the Liberty Bowl of 1982. When Bryant retired in 1982 with 323 victories, his achievements made him college football's most successful coach ever. That record has since been broken but by coaches who took several more years of coaching than Bryant used to establish it.

**Left: Joe Namath (12, dark helmet) directed Alabama to a 10-1 season as a sophomore in 1962.**

**Right: Coach Bryant is carried off the field after Alabama beat Mississippi 12-7 in the 1964 Sugar Bowl.**

Bryant earned his success. He drilled his Alabama teams just as he had drilled that 1954 Texas A&M squad. He never believed in using tricky offenses or a sack full of gadget plays. Instead, he established his style of football first by constructing rock-solid defenses, and then added a very basic but mistake-free offense that was not hard to figure out, yet was so well drilled that it was tough to contain.

Bryant, always a practical coach, kept an open mind about strategy. "People win games, not formations," he claimed. During most of the sixties, his Alabama teams had a coterie of fine passers in Pat Trammell, Joe Namath, Steve Sloan, Ken Stabler, and Scott Hunter. So he used a solid mix of running and passing to forge his success. In the late sixties and seventies, the Wishbone became the fashionable offense and Bryant recruited quarterbacks who were more suited to that style. Unlike most pure "bone" teams, he kept a passing game that gave his offense an extra dimension.

Bryant's first season produced a 5-4-1 record and Tide followers breathed a sigh of relief at the positive results. Bryant notched his 100th

career win in 1959 over Tulane in quarterback Bobby Skelton's first start and it became like old times at the Capstone when the Tide returned to the post-season in the inaugural Liberty Bowl in Philadelphia. Though he lost to Penn State 7-0 on a fake field goal-touchdown pass, Bryant had brought his team back to respectability in just two seasons as the 1959 team forged a 7-1-2 record.

The rebirth of Alabama football was completed two years later in 1961 when he won the national championship. He deftly used a two-quarterback system with Skelton as a skilled passer and Pat

**Left: Bryant called Joe Namath "the best athlete I've ever seen." In his senior year, with the help of Steve Sloan, Namath led the Tide to a national championship.**

**Above: Bryant with QB Steve Sloan after winning the 1966 Orange Bowl and another national championship.**

Trammell offering better running ability and superb leadership. Bryant's defense allowed just 25 total points, the fewest ever by a Bryant-coached team, and shut out its last five regular season opponents. A decisive 34-0 final game victory over Auburn clinched the national championship. Alabama then capped its first perfect season since 1945 by beating Arkansas 10-3 in the Sugar Bowl.

Joe Namath became Bryant's quarterback in 1962 and before his career at Alabama ended in 1964—and long before he became a hero to members of the Age of Aquarius as the $400,000 quarterback of the New York Jets—Bryant would call him "the best athlete I've ever seen, blessed with that rare quickness—hands, feet, everything."

Namath fired a 52-yard touchdown pass to end Richard Williamson on the fifth play of his varsity career in 1962, and he ended that 10-1 season with the same play in a 17-0 Orange Bowl victory over Oklahoma. Though Namath became a hero of sorts to the counter-culturists of the sixties, Bryant showed him no special treatment. He even suspended him for the last two games of the 1963 season against Miami and a Sugar Bowl date against Mississippi, for violating team rules. Alabama won both games with Jack Hurlbut and Steve

**Left: Bryant and his famed left-handed quarterback, Ken Stabler.**

**Above: Ken (The Snake) Stabler in action against Nebraska in the 1967 Sugar Bowl.**

**Right: Hardhitting defense, which caused opponents to fumble, was the hallmark of Bryant's teams, as in this game against Mississippi in 1967.**

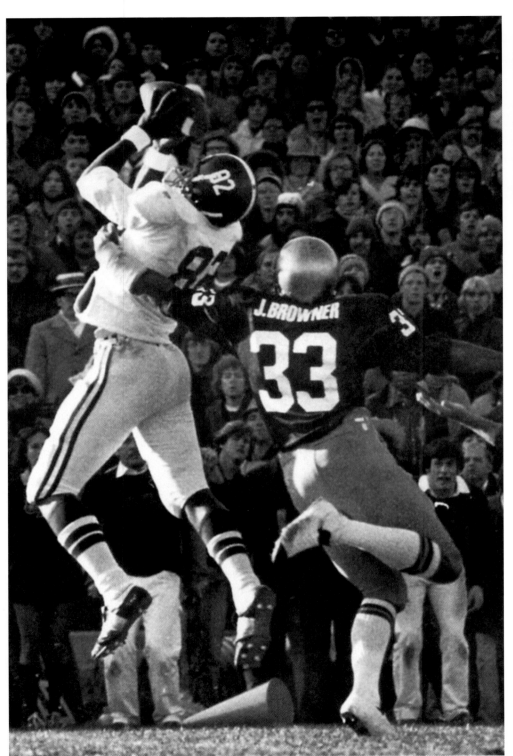

Left: Ozzie Newsome (82) takes to the air to haul in a pass on the Notre Dame 9-yard line late in the fourth quarter of the Notre Dame-Alabama game in 1976.

Above: Alabama's Tyrone King (43) makes an airborne interception of a pass intended for Georgia's Lynn Hunnicut (84) en route to a 25-7 victory in 1972.

Right: Bryant gives instructions from his daily perch in "the tower."

Sloan at quarterback, surprising even Bryant. "But after I got to thinking about it, I said, 'Shoot, you can do anything if you want to badly enough,'" Bryant said later.

A knee injury in the fourth game of the 1964 season forced Namath to the bench, but Alabama still won the national championship. When he was healthy enough to play, Namath shared time with Steve Sloan. Sloan did the passing in long-yardage situations because of Namath's limited mobility. Ray Ogden's 107-yard kickoff return keyed a 21-14 Thanksgiving Day victory over Auburn and three days later top-ranked Notre Dame lost to Southern Cal, giving Bryant and the Tide their second national title.

Sloan ably stepped in and produced a 9-1-1 record in 1965 that was climaxed by a rollicking 39-28 victory on New Year's Day over Nebraska in the 1966 Orange Bowl. The Tide was ranked No. 4 when the day began, but the three teams ranked ahead of them all lost, giving Alabama the third national title during Bryant's reign.

Bryant should have made it four in a row with an undefeated team in 1966. He called it "my uncrowned champions," and "the greatest college football team I've ever seen or been associated with," declaring also that it was better than his '65 champions. But college football's pollsters were so roiled by the late season 10-10 tie played by 1-2 ranked Notre Dame and Michigan State, they overlooked the Tide. Neither played a post-season game while Alabama walloped Nebraska 34-7 in the Sugar Bowl. The pollsters didn't budge and the Tide's 12-0 record meant only a No. 3 ranking.

The Age of the Wishbone arrived in 1969 and Bryant greeted it with a great running back in Johnny Musso. Nicknamed the "Italian Stallion," he broke all of Alabama's major rushing records during his three seasons, finishing his career with 2,741 yards and 34 touchdowns, 16 in his 1971 senior season. He still ranks No. 3 in career rushing behind Shaun Alexander (3,565) and Bobby Humphrey (3,420).

Another 11-1 season in 1973 made it a fourth national title for Bryant. Paced by quarterbacks Richard Todd and Gary Rutledge, and running back Wilbur Jackson, this Alabama team rolled up a school record 477 points. Though Alabama lost to top-ranked (AP) Notre Dame 24-23 in the Sugar Bowl, it still was crowned the nation's team by UPI.

Bryant got his two final national titles in 1978 and 1979. The 11-1 team in 1978 was led by Jeff Rutledge's record 30 touchdown passes. It lost only to Southern Cal but clinched the national title with a 14-7 win in the Sugar Bowl against Penn State, helped by a tremendous late-game goal-line stand that prevented the tying score.

**Above: QB Jeff Rutledge led the Tide to its 1978 national championship.**

**Right: QB Terry Davis (10) ran Alabama's Wishbone offense superbly and led the Tide to a pair of SEC titles in 1971-72.**

**Right:** Steadman Shealy
(with ball) quarterbacked
Bryant's final national
championship team in 1979.

His 1979 team was a unanimous selection as national champion after its 12-0 season, helped by timely big plays by several players and a top-ranked scoring defense. Running back Major Ogilvie scored twice as the Tide overcame a 17-0 deficit to beat Tennessee 27-17; Alan McElroy kicked a 27-yard field goal in the third quarter for a 3-0 win against LSU; quarterback Steadman Shealy's eight-yard touchdown run secured a 25-18 victory over Auburn in the season's finale; and the defense stopped Arkansas six times on the third down in the Sugar Bowl to preserve a 24-9 victory. When top-ranked Ohio State lost in the Rose Bowl, Bryant got his final national title.

His final target was Amos Alonzo Stagg's all-time record of 314 victories. Bryant was 66 when he won his last national title. Some wondered if he had the stamina to continue, but that was never an issue with the Bear. He got victory Number 300 early in 1980; tied Number 2 Glenn (Pop) Warner's record of 313 wins in 1981 against Mississippi State on Terry Sander's fourth field goal; and then tied Stagg's record the following week with a 36-16 triumph over Penn State and coach Joe Paterno. (Ironically, nearly a quarter century later, Paterno broke Bryant's ultimate record of 323 victories.)

Two weeks later in Alabama's final game of the 1981 season against archrival Auburn, Bryant broke Stagg's record with a come-from-behind 28-17 victory, keyed by Walter Lewis's 38-yard touchdown pass to Jesse Bendross.

Bryant returned for a final season in 1982, and his team struggled to win eight of 12 games. The final victory came, as previously noted, in the Liberty Bowl against Illinois.

So it was that after 25 years at the Capstone, Bear Bryant quietly exited the Alabama football stage for good. Many had wondered what he would do in retirement without a football team to coach and lead to victory. But fate intervened: a month after coaching his final game, Bear Bryant died suddenly.

**Opposite: Bear Bryant's funeral procession on January 28, 1983, passes by the stadium that now bears his name, where he won 72 games.**

**Above: A huge display of roses marks Bear Bryant's final resting place.**

**Right: Bear Bryant in a most familiar pre-game pose.**

# 6

# 'BAMA BEAT ROLLS ON

For the last few years prior to Coach Bear Bryant's retirement, the most dreaded question around the Capstone was, "Who's going to replace the Bear?" The correct answer was, "No one."

Of course, that was the heart of Alabama football speaking.

The ultimate solution was the same one that brought Bryant to Alabama 25 years earlier: Find a talented coach who had Alabama roots and hire him.

Hello, Ray Perkins!

Perkins had been a fine offensive end for Bryant and was a member of Alabama's 1965 national champions. He was a seventh round draft choice of the Baltimore Colts in 1966 and became an NFL assistant coach after his playing career ended. In 1979, he was named head coach of the New York Giants and late in the 1982 season, while in his fourth season as their coach, he was picked to succeed Bryant.

Claiming that "coaching Alabama's football team is the only job I really ever wanted," he immediately resigned from the Giants though the team was contending for a second straight playoff spot and had only two games left in the 1982 season. The Giants split the games and missed the playoffs.

Those next four years with Perkins in charge were nerve-wracking for Tide fans.

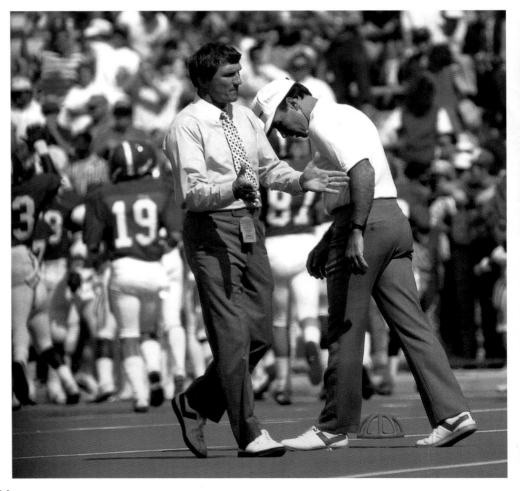

Right: Ray Perkins (shirt and tie), who played on Bear Bryant's 1964-65 national champions, had the impossible task of replacing the most legendary coach in Alabama history. Constantly reminded that he was "no Bear Bryant," Perkins lasted four seasons but guided the Tide to three post-season games.

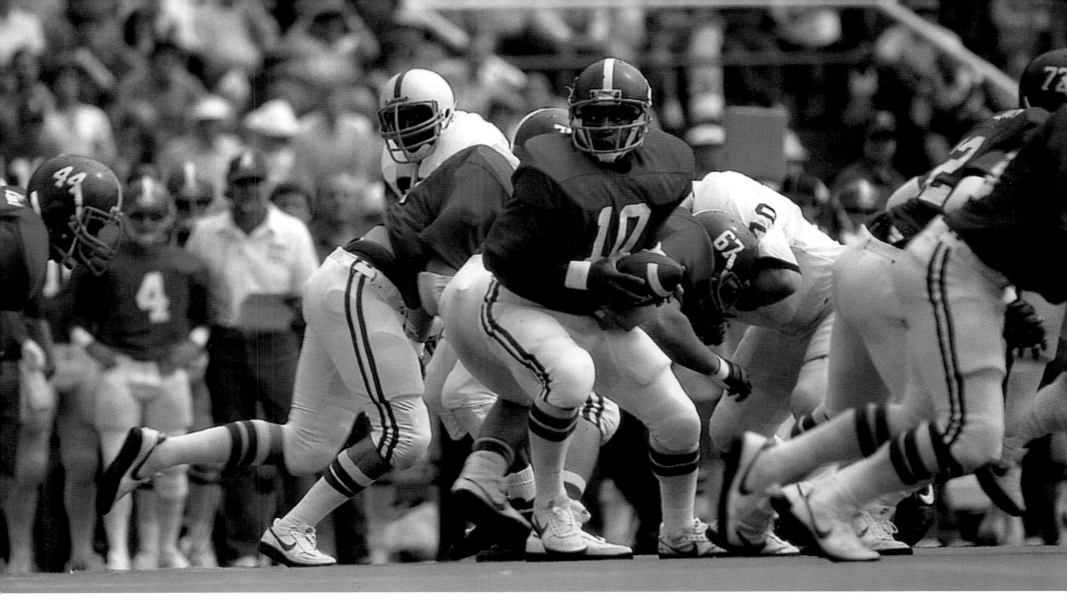

Above: QB Walter Lewis led Alabama in passing in 1981-83 and ranks sixth in Tide history with 4257 yards.

Left: For over a half-century, Alabama's mascot has been the Red Elephant.

Right: Sellout crowds fill both Legion Field in Birmingham and Bryant-Denny Stadium in Tuscaloosa for every game.

Right: Quarterback Walter Lewis was Alabama's best all-around offensive performer during the 1980s. He led the team to three postseason games and an SEC title. His 2329 total yards in 1983 ranks No. 2 in Alabama history.

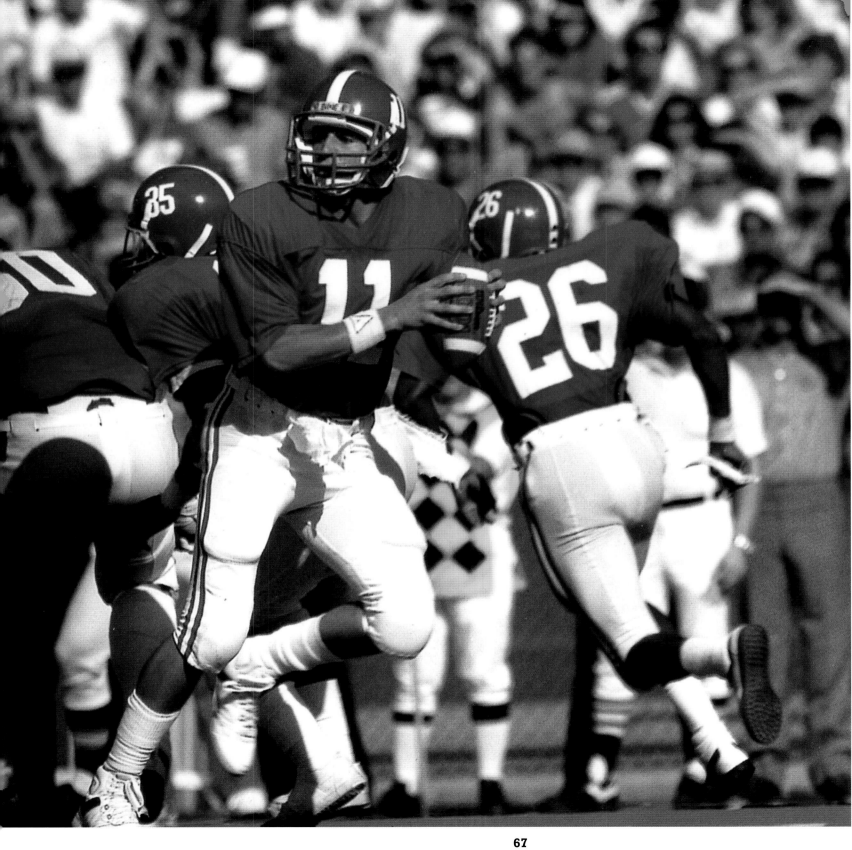

Left: David Shula, son of the famed NFL coach, led Alabama's passers in both 1985 and 1986 and threw 29 TD passes during those seasons.

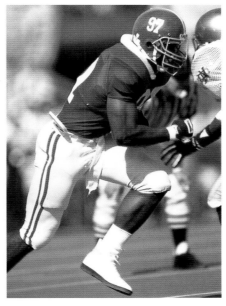

Being asked to succeed an icon like Bryant was a singular honor for Perkins, but after the buzz wore off came the realization that replacing someone long considered irreplaceable is a no-win situation. The successor really is never good enough in the eyes of the fans and pundits because he can never measure up to the "legend."

That's how it was with Perkins. His 32-15-1 record over four seasons would have been applauded at most schools but not at one that was dogged by the ghost of Bear Bryant. His teams won all three bowl games to which they were invited, but they never came close to winning a national championship. Alabama's highest poll ranking during his tenure was ninth place in his final season (1986), but in 1984 he also suffered the team's first losing season since 1957. Bryant, of course, never had a losing season and had won the first of six national championships in his fourth season.

Perkins, a stoic, all-business coach in contrast to Bryant's "aw-shucks, down-home" approach, finished his first season with a 7-4 record, the same as the Bear's final season. Perkins's chief weapon was quarterback Walter Lewis, a superb runner who rang up a school record of 2,329 yards of total offense.

Perkins won his first four games, including a 20-7 opener over Georgia Tech. Ironically, Tech's coach was a former Colts teammate, Bill Curry, who succeeded Perkins as Alabama's head coach four years later. A 34-28 loss to Penn State in the fifth game was followed by a 41-34 loss to Tennessee when the Vols outscored the Tide 10-0 in the fourth quarter. That ended his Alabama honeymoon.

The season ended well in the Sun Bowl when the Tide scored 28 points in the first half and Ricky Moore had his sixth consecutive 100-yard rushing game as Alabama upset Southern Methodist, 28-7. But the loss to Tennessee, a fierce rival, began a disturbing pattern of blown

**Left: Van Tiffin kicked a record 135 consecutive extra points for Alabama, plus 59 field goals, and ranks third in all-time scoring with 312 points. Here he kicks one of those field goals against Ohio State in the 1986 Kickoff Classic during a 16-10 victory.**

**Above: Cornelius Bennett was one of the finest linebackers ever to play at Alabama.**

late game leads throughout Perkins's tenure that triggered constant "that didn't happen when Bear was here" grumbling.

It didn't help, either, that Alabama got off to a horrible start in 1984, losing four of its first five games, suffering its first losing season since 1957. Worse still, four of its six losses that year occurred after the Tide was ahead in the fourth quarter, one of them again being archrival Tennessee in the final eight minutes of a 28-27 loss.

The season's bright spots were on defense. Linebackers Cornelius Bennett and Wayne Davis each had ten tackles and Van Tiffen kicked a pair of fourth quarter field goals in a 6-0 victory over Penn State while freshman defensive back Rory Turner's fourth down tackle at the one-yard line in the final second preserved a heroic 17-15 victory over Auburn.

The roller-coaster ride continued in 1985. In the opening game against Georgia, the Tide trailed by three points with 50 seconds to play and won the game when David Shula passed to Al Bell for the winning score with 15 seconds left; then in the finale of their 9-2-1 season, Tiffin kicked the winning field goal against Auburn with no time left. The Tide ended the season with a 24-3 win against Southern Cal in the Aloha Bowl.

Perkins's last season in 1986 was another series of heart-stopping wins and losses. The Tide was ranked second after a 7-0 start, then lost three of its last five games, beginning with a 23-3 loss to eventual national champion Penn State. It finished ninth in the final poll ranking. But the Tide also had a first-ever win over Notre Dame as Shula threw three touchdown passes in a 28-10 victory.

A new running star, sophomore Bobby Humphrey, flashed onto the scene. He gained 217 rushing yards and scored three touchdowns in a resounding 56-28 victory over Tennessee. Two weeks later he had 284 yards and three touchdowns against Mississippi. When his career ended three seasons later, he was the school's all-time rusher with 3,420 yards. That record lasted until Shaun Alexander set the current mark of 3,565 in 1999.

Alabama blew a 17-7 lead in the fourth quarter against Auburn in the season's final game and lost 21-17. Even though his team had one of its greatest performances during Perkins's four-season tenure in beating Washington 28-6 in the Sun Bowl, it didn't quiet the discontented Alabama fans, and

**Right: Bill Curry served as Alabama coach from 1987-89.**

**Opposite: Alabama's defense has always been taught to swarm to a ball carrier and John Mangum (29), Steve Webb (84), and Charles Gardner do it against Tennessee during the Tide's victory over the Vols in 1989.**

Perkins left, albeit in good shape with a multi-million dollar contract to coach the NFL's Tampa Bay Buccaneers. That left the football program still seeking the stability that Bryant had brought it during his quarter-century as head coach.

There were two obvious options for Alabama—find someone with an Alabama background, as had happened with previous Alabama coaching hires, or go outside, which hadn't happened since Wallace Wade was hired in 1923.

In a drastic departure, Alabama decided to go outside its family and chose Bill Curry, who had never played or coached at Alabama. As noted earlier in this chapter, he had been head coach at Georgia Tech and had an extensive playing career at Baltimore and Green Bay of the NFL. But his lack of Alabama roots always worked against him, and despite producing an excellent 25-10 record, Alabama fans never fully accepted him.

His one great asset in 1987 was Humphrey, who gained 220 rushing yards to key a 24-13 win over Penn State; he scored the winning touchdown with 46 seconds to play in the Tide's 21-18 win over Mississippi State the week after he raked Tennessee for 127 yards in a decisive 41-22 victory. In one of his most dominating performances ever, he gained 177 yards when Alabama kept the ball for 40 minutes against LSU and came from behind to win, 22-10. That seemed to be forgotten after archrival Auburn defeated Alabama 10-0 and Michigan came from behind and beat the Tide 28-24 in the final minutes of the Hall of Fame Bowl.

When Humphrey was lost for the last seven games of the 1988 season, the defense had to take over. Linebacker Derrick Thomas, following in the footsteps of Cornelius Bennett, was a tremendous force. He had five sacks in a 30-10 victory over Texas A&M; eight tackles, three sacks, one for a safety and constant harassment of Penn State's quarterback in the Tide's scrappy 8-3 victory; and 14 tackles, four sacks, a blocked punt, and a recovered fumble in beating Kentucky 31-17.

The Tide beat Tennessee 28-20 with 98 seconds to play on Murry Hill's 55-yard touchdown run, and it contained Army's devastating Wishbone attack and won the Sun Bowl 29-28 by scoring nine points in the fourth quarter.

**Opposite: Bobby Humphrey was a prolific ground-gainer with 3420 yards in four seasons, including four games of more than 200 yards that includes 284 yards against Mississippi State in 1986, the one-best on-game performance in Tide history.**

**Right: Derrick Thomas continued a long tradition of great Tide linebackers that included Leroy Jordan and Cornelius Bennett. Thomas had tremendous speed from sideline-to-sideline and starred in the NFL until he was killed in an auto accident while still at the peak of his career.**

Alabama won its first ten games of the 1989 season and contended for the national title until being upset 30-20, by 11th ranked Auburn. That loss also cost it the SEC title which, coupled with a loss to eventual national champion Miami, sealed Curry's fate at Alabama. He left early in 1990 to become head coach at Kentucky, leaving Alabama to continue its search for football coaching happiness.

# 7

# IN THE BEAR'S IMAGE

Alabama's fans had made it clear during the Bill Curry era that they wanted no part of any head coach who didn't have a Capstone pedigree, just as they had demonstrated quite strongly during the previous Ray Perkins era that while they preferred a Bear Bryant-trained coach, he had better be a winner.

So they got their wish on both counts when Gene Stallings was hired to replace Curry. The result? When Stallings left Alabama after the 1996 season, those fans knew they had come as close as they ever could to seeing the reincarnation of their beloved Bear.

Before coming to Alabama, Stallings had been influenced by two great coaches during his football career—Bryant and Tom Landry. So there was no disputing his football heritage. He had played end for The Bear at Texas A&M from 1954-56 and immediately caught Bryant's attention at his infamous 1954 "boot camp" with his toughness and devotion to the game. Bryant thought so highly of him that he named him a tri-captain of the Aggies' undefeated 1956 national championship team, and then hired him as an assistant coach the following year. He accompanied Bryant to Alabama in 1958 as an assistant coach and worked for him until being hired in 1965 as head coach at his alma mater. He coached the Aggies for seven years (1965-71) and then joined the incomparable Landry in 1972 for another 14 seasons as an assistant with the Dallas Cowboys.

**Opposite:** Toderick Malone produces a big play that helped Alabama defeat LSU 22-16, one of the Tide's easier victories during its 12-1 1994 season.

**Left:** David Palmer, after eluding four would-be tacklers, finishes a 52-yard first-quarter punt return for a touchdown in the 1991 Blockbuster Bowl versus Colorado. It gave the Tide a 7-0 lead en route to a 30-15 victory and helped Palmer to win the Brian Piccolo Award as the game's MVP.

**Above:** Alabama tried to revive the Bear Bryant legend by hiring one of his former pupils and coaches, Gene Stallings, as head coach in 1990. Stallings had played for him at Texas A&M and was an Alabama assistant coach during the 1960s.

**Right: Defensive back George Teague celebrates with his mates after returning an interception for a touchdown in the 1992 Sugar Bowl, which helped defeat top-ranked Miami on the way to winning the national championship.**

**Opposite: Alabama players give their head coach Gene Stallings a victory ride after defeating Miami in the 1992 Sugar Bowl and winning the Tide's first national championship since 1979.**

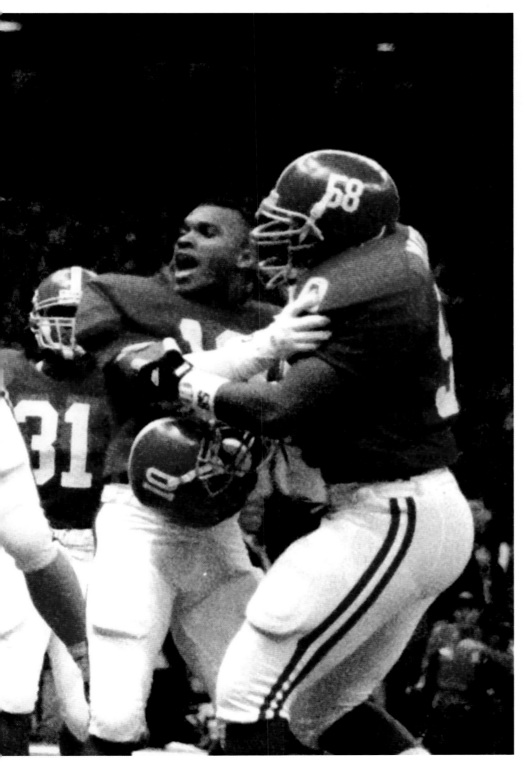

Stallings, who never played pro football, became head coach of the St. Louis Football Cardinals in 1986 and stayed with them for three full seasons, including the last two in St. Louis before the team moved to Phoenix in 1988. He resigned with five games remaining in the 1989 season.

Alabama, still longing for another Bryant "type" of head coach, made a splendid choice when it hired Stallings in 1990. In his second year at the Capstone, he won 11 of 12 games. The following year, he came as close as was possible to reincarnating Bryant when his team celebrated the centennial of Alabama football as the 12th team at Alabama to win a national championship with its 12-0 season. His 1994 team also had a 12-1 record. His official seven-season record is 62-25, third winningest in the school's history behind Bryant and Frank Thomas.

But there is another set of numbers—his actual on-the-field record of 70-16-1—that tells a different story of his time at Alabama and underscores the controversy that seemed to dog him. That official record became

62-25-0 after the NCAA charged Alabama with using an illegal player, defensive back Antonio Langham, during its 9-3-1 season in 1993 and forced the Tide to forfeit every victory and the tie in which Langham had appeared. That lowered its record that season to 1-12.

Some background: A few hours after the 1992 team had defeated Miami in the Sugar Bowl and clinched the national championship, Langham made a verbal agreement with an agent and affixed his signature to a cocktail napkin to seal the deal. NCAA rules forbid players who wish to retain playing eligibility to sign with agents, and Langham still had another year of eligibility when he did so.

Stallings didn't find out about Langham's actions, which should have negated any further playing eligibility, until late in the 1993 season. He immediately suspended him for games, against Auburn and the SEC championship game against Florida. The Tide lost both games, but Stallings did not report the incident to the NCAA.

It wasn't until prior to the 1995 season that NCAA investigators discovered that Langham's action was one of several violations in Alabama's athletic program. Stallings, along with athletic director Hootie Ingram, were implicated in falsifying Langham's eligibility during the 1993 season. Alabama was banned from post-season play in 1995; lost 22 athletic scholarships in 1995-96; was placed on three years' probation; and was ordered to forfeit all games in which Langham had participated in 1993. Hence, the official 1993 record became 1-12 instead of 9-3-1.

None of that had yet impacted the Tide, because in 1994 Stallings's team had a magnificent 12-1 record and a fifth-place national ranking. This was one of his grittiest teams because six of its victories were by a touchdown or less, including a 13-6 victory over Arkansas; a 29-28 win against Georgia when quarterback Jay Barker completed 26 of 34 passes for 396 yards and wide receiver Toderick Malone caught nine of his passes for 173 yards and two touchdowns; a 14-6 triumph over upstart Southern Mississippi; a 29-25 victory over Mississippi State; a 17-13 win against Tennessee; and a 21-14 victory over Auburn. Its only loss was 24-23 for the SEC title against Florida. The Tide then defeated Ohio State 24-17 in the Citrus Bowl.

Toughness and defense were hallmarks of Stallings's teams, beginning with his first season in 1990 when the Tide lost its first three games,

**Right: Jay Barker's grittiness as a quarterback typified the style of play by his team in 1994 when Alabama won six regular season games by a touchdown or less before losing its final game, in the SEC championship, to Florida by one point. The Tide then defeated Ohio State in the Citrus Bowl, 24-17.**

**Opposite: QB Jay Barker gets the national TV treatment after completing 26 of 34 passes for 396 yards in a 29-28 victory over Georgia.**

then won seven of its final eight by allowing just three touchdowns and reached the Fiesta Bowl. Would-be critics, who had a field day against Perkins and Curry, were muted when Phil Doyle kicked a 48-yard field goal on the game's final play to defeat Tennessee 9-6; they later beat archrival Auburn, 16-7.

Tide fans knew that Stallings was the real deal in 1991when his team bounced back from a 35-0 loss to Florida in the season's second game

**Opposite: Defense Alabama-style means a gang-tackling, no-holds barred job against Auburn during the Tide's 21-14 victory in 1994.**

**Above: Opposing quarterbacks Patrick Nix of Auburn (left) and 'Bama's Jay Barker meet after Barker led the Tide to a 21-14 victory in the 1994 annual Iron Bowl.**

**Right: Wide receiver Curtis Brown (85) and Jay Barker (7) were a productive tandem during Alabama's 24-17 victory over Ohio State in the Citrus Bowl, capping a 12-1 1994 season.**

and never lost again. Alabama was behind 6-3 going into the final quarter against Tennessee but Siran Stacy scored two touchdowns as the Tide outscored the Vols 21-13 to grab a 24-19 victory. Two weeks later at LSU, Alabama had a 20-7 halftime when David Palmer returned a punt 90 yards for a touchdown and redshirt freshman quarterback Jay Barker made a successful debut. Still, it took Antonio London's third blocked field goal of the season in the final two minutes to preserve the 20-17 win.

Barker scored the game's only touchdown as Alabama defeated Auburn 13-6 for its tenth win of the season, the 22nd such milestone in its history, and an NCAA record. A few weeks later, the Tide defeated Colorado 30-25 in the

**Right:** Darrell Blackburn and Ralph Staten (41) epitomize the fierce play of 'Bama's defense and get after Ohio State quarterback Bobby Hoying during the Tide's 24-17 victory in the 2005 Citrus Bowl.

**Opposite:** The Tide's Sherman Williams cranks up Alabama's running game during its 17-13 victory over archrival Tennessee.

**Opposite Right:** The time-honored and traditional victory cigars get a good workout from quarterback Jay Barker and head coach Gene Stallings following Alabama's 1994 victory over Tennessee.

Blockbuster II Bowl, its record 44th bowl game. Palmer scored twice, on his fourth touchdown punt return of the season and on Barker's third touchdown pass of the game with 6:50 to play for the ultimate victory margin.

Of course, the crown jewel of Stallings's tenure was the 1992 national championship season. Once more, the Tide's success centered around its defense, which many still claim was one of the greatest in modern college football history. Ranked first in the nation, it shut out three opponents and never allowed more than 21 points (twice). It held Southern Mississippi to just 54 yards and three first downs (one on a penalty, none by passing) in a 17-10 victory. The Tide's 17-10 victory over Tennessee, its seventh in a row against the Vols, was saved by a last-minute interception.

Alabama polished off the regular season by winning the first SEC championship game—and its 20th conference title—with a 28-21 victory over Florida when Langham returned an interception 27 yards for a touchdown with three minutes to play. Derrick Lassic scored two touchdowns and Barker threw a 30-yard touchdown pass to Curtis Brown for the other scores.

Alabama, ranked second at the end of the regular season, played top-ranked Miami in the Sugar Bowl and Stallings simply relied on what had succeeded—defense and running—for a solid 34-13 victory. The defense held Miami to 48 rushing yards and broke open a close game early in the second half when interceptions by Tommy Johnson and George Teague helped to produce two touchdowns. The Tide's offense churned out 267 rushing yards with Lassic getting 135 and two touchdowns.

Stallings's final season in 1996 produced a 10-3 record and another trip to the SEC championship game. But on November 23, 1996, two weeks before the game, he announced that he was resigning at the end of the season and the letdown on the team was palpable. The Tide defense, particularly, seemed to be most affected and simply played without any emotion in losing to Florida, 45-30.

But Stallings didn't allow the players to use his leaving as an excuse for any further failure, and he had Alabama at peak form in its 17-14 victory over Michigan in the Outback Bowl.

That's how the Bear would have done it. That's how his prime pupil did it, too.

Opposite: Alabama defender Chris Hood stops a Michigan running back during the Tide's 17-14 victory in the 1996 Outback Bowl.

Left: Defensive back Kevin Jackson (7) and defensive mates battle Michigan quarterback for the loose football during the 1996 Outback Bowl. The Tide's 17-14 victory was the last game coached by Gene Stallings.

# 8

# A ROLLERCOASTER ERA

The cozy, comfortable world that had been Alabama football for most of the 20th century had begun to fray at the edges after Bear Bryant left in 1983. Gene Stallings restored some of the greatness with his 1992 national championship team and with his superb teams in 1991, 1994, and 1996. After that, football life at the Capstone suddenly became very iffy.

In seeking a successor to Stallings, as usual, the Tide looked to one of its own, tapping his defensive coordinator Mike DuBose for the top job. DuBose was Alabama football through-and-through. He was one of the team's top defensive players while playing for Bryant in the mid-70s (1972-74) when the Tide posted an overall record of 32-4, won a national championship and three conference titles.

A native of Opp, Alabama, DuBose returned to his alma mater as defensive line coach on Ray Perkins's staff in 1983, and when Perkins left Alabama to coach the NFL's Tampa Bay Buccaneers, he went with him. Three seasons later, he was back at Alabama coaching the defensive line for Stallings and was named defensive coordinator in 1996, Stallings's final season.

DuBose was a fiery, determined player, and was a very effective assistant coach, particularly during the 90s when Stallings's teams were so successful on defense. He was one of the

**Right: Coach Mike DuBose, who played for Bear Bryant at Alabama and was the team's defensive coordinator under Gene Stallings, climaxed his second season as Alabama's head coach in 1998 with a victory over archrival Auburn in the Iron Bowl.**

**Opposite: Shaun Alexander was the most explosive running back in Alabama football history. He's the school's all-time leader with 15 games in which he gained over 100 yards, including the 1999 SEC championship game against Florida where he also scored four rushing touchdowns.**

architects of the 1992 team's rushing defense that was ranked No. 1 nationally. Ten of his players achieved all-conference or All-America status, and five of them became NFL first round draft picks.

Thus, Tide followers had every right to expect that the successes they had experienced under Stallings would continue. What they failed to take into account was the effect of losing 22 football scholarships in 1995-96. This had severely depleted the team's playing depth and overall talent pool. Nor was there any guarantee that a fine assistant coach would also become an equally effective head coach.

The DuBose era started with a lackluster 6-5 record in 1997, where a 4-1 start was sullied by an 0-3 finish that included a 27-0 loss to LSU, 32-20 to Mississippi State, and 18-17 to Auburn.

The 1998 season was a bit better at 7-5, including victories over LSU and Auburn. The Tide had also begun to showcase the tremendous playing talents of junior running back Shaun Alexander, quarterback Andrew Zow, and wide receiver Freddie Milons. This trio became one of the most formidable offensive forces in Alabama football history in 1998 and 1999.

Alexander flashed onto the scene in the 1998 season's opening game against Brigham Young when he scored a school record five touchdowns in a 38-31 victory (a record later tied by wide receiver Santonio Beard in 2002 against Ole Miss). In the season's most exhilarating win, 22-16 over LSU, Alexander and Zow keyed a fourth-quarter comeback for a 22-16 victory. Behind 16-7, they combined for a 22-yard touchdown pass; and with 38 seconds to play, Zow passed 25 yards for the winning score to Quincy Jackson and added a two-point P.A.T. with a pass to Michael Vaughn.

Alexander, 5'11" running back from Florence, Kentucky, about an hour's drive from SEC rival Kentucky, was the linchpin of Alabama's offense during his four varsity seasons, from 1996 to 1999. When he finished his career, he owned nearly every important rushing record, including the all-time career marks of 3,565 yards and 41 touchdowns. Against Louisiana State in 1996, he averaged 14.6 yards per carry in gaining 291 yards, both Alabama records. The five rushing touchdowns he scored against Brigham Young in 1998 tied an Alabama record. In 1999, he rewrote the school's single-season scoring records with 144 points on 24 touchdowns, both records. His 19 rushing touchdowns that season were a school record.

**Right: Shaun Alexander flashed onto Alabama's football scene in 1998 and underscored his great talent against LSU when he and QB Andrew Zow combined to produce 16 fourth-quarter points for a 22-16 victory.**

**Opposite: Alabama wide receiver Santonio Beard steps into the end zone with one of his five record-setting touchdowns during a 2002 victory over Ole Miss.**

In 1999, he had a four-touchdown (24 points) game against Florida in a season-ending 34-7 victory. The week before against Auburn he was never better. He scored three fourth-quarter touchdowns to bring the Tide from a 14-8 deficit to a 28-17 victory and amassed 198 rushing yards on 33 carries.

The Tide rebounded for an 8-3 record in 1999 and a berth in the 2000 Orange Bowl, where they lost 35-34 in overtime to Michigan because of a missed extra point following Antonio Carter's 21-yard touchdown pass from Zow. The Alexander-Zow-Milons troika was magnificent in that game. Alexander rushed for 161 yards and scored a school bowl record three touchdowns, the last one on a 50-yard run. Milons set a school and bowl punt return record with 107 yards, including one of 60 yards for a touchdown.

Zow, just a sophomore in 1999, improved every season. He ranks second in every major category on Alabama's career-passing list, not bad considering that the list includes such Tide quarterback stars as Joe Namath, Harry Gilmer, Jay Barker, Brodie Croyle, and Walter Lewis. His career totals include 459 completions for 5,983

**Opposite: QB Andrew Zow not only was a fine passing quarterback at Alabama with over 5,983 career yards, but he also excelled as an option quarterback, which he demonstrated during a Tide victory over Ole Miss.**

**Left: Zow finished his career at Alabama ranked No. 2, both in pass completions with 459 and total offense with 5,958 yards.**

**Above: Wide receiver Freddie Milons scorched Florida for ten catches in 1999 en route to a season total of 65, his best at Alabama. He finished his career as the school's all-time receiver with 152 catches and is second in receiving yards with 1,859.**

yards and 35 touchdowns. Further, in each of his final three seasons, he threw three touchdowns in three different games; and he has the Tide's all-time consecutive completion streak with 12 in a row against Florida in 2000.

Milons was truly Mr. Excitement in Alabama's passing game during his four seasons and finished his career as the Tide's all-time receiver with 152 catches. His 1,859 yards ranks second to Ozzie Newsome's 2,070. Milons's best season was 1999 when he caught 65 passes for 733 yards. Three times during his career he had games in which he caught nine passes, in 1999 against Mississippi (133 yards) and Mississippi State (94 yards) and in 2000 against South Carolina. His best catching day came in 1999 against Florida when he caught ten passes for 119 yards.

With Alexander gone, the 2000 season was book-ended by losses in three of the Tide's first four games, and all of its last five for a 3-8 record, its poorest in 43 years. Worse still, reported problems in DuBose's personal life also became an issue throughout the season. At first he denied the reports, but as the cloud around him began to grow and the team started to disintegrate, he admitted to their validity and announced, with three games to play, that he would leave Alabama at the end of the season.

But more serious problems beset Alabama's football program. For the second time in less than ten years, the NCAA

**Below: In 2001, Dennis Franchione became the first Crimson Tide head coach without an Alabama "pedigree" since Wallace Wade took the job in 1923. Though hampered by a lack of football scholarships because Alabama was in the midst of a five-year NCAA probation, Franchione compiled a respectable 17-8 record during his two seasons as head coach.**

**Right: Wide receiver Freddie Milons caught nine passes in a game a record three times during his career, one of those against South Carolina in 2000.**

**Opposite: Milons had a record 10-catch game against Florida during the SEC championship game in 1999. He also finished his career with four games during which he gained more than 100 yards from pass receptions.**

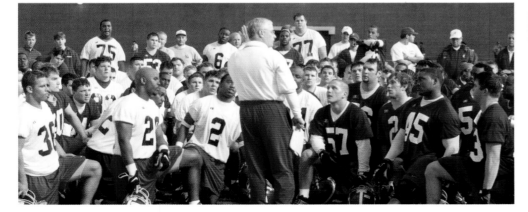

found the school had violated recruiting rules and slapped it with a two-year ban against post-season play; took away 21 scholarships over three years (2003-05); and put the program on five years probation.

While that was transpiring, the search began for a new coach, and this time Alabama deviated from its "homegrown" candidate and hired Dennis Franchione, who had never coached or played one down of football in the state of Alabama. Still, he was considered the best of nearly two dozen Division 1-A head-coaching candidates who were available for jobs that year.

"I didn't know if I would ever be identified as a guy who could go into the SEC or the south, not having many ties back there," he said later. "But when Alabama calls, you get excited, there's no doubt about that."

**Left:** Ahmad Galloway (No. 29 with ball) en route to making a big play in the 2001 Independence Bowl against Iowa State. The Tide pulled out a 14-13 victory in the game that capped a furious season-ending rush during which it won its last four games.

**Above:** Freddie Milons also excelled as a punt and kickoff return specialist as he demonstrated against Iowa State in the 2001 Independence Bowl. His 917 career kickoff return yards ranks third in school history.

Certainly, Franchione found Alabama a different world than that in which he had lived while spending most of his career coaching in the Southwest, particularly at Texas Christian University. But after two seasons, during which his Alabama teams compiled a 17-8 record, including 10-3 in 2002, he grabbed an opportunity to return "home" to Texas and coach Texas A&M.

The 2001 team shrugged off a three-game, mid-season losing streak and won its last three games for a 6-5 record. That was good enough for a spot in the Independence Bowl, where it defeated Iowa State 14-13.

In 2002, the team won six of its last seven games, including a 21-11 "visit" to Hawaii, obviously in lieu of the bowl game that it was not allowed to attend. The season's key victory was 34-14 over Tennessee. Earlier, it had been revealed that Vols head coach Phil Fullmer was a "secret witness" in the NCAA investigation that put Alabama on its most recent probation. Thus, a heated rivalry became white hot on the field, resulting in 19 penalties, eleven against the Tide. Alabama's defense intercepted three passes, posted four sacks, and got a 66-yard fumble recovery by Gerald Dixon for a touchdown.

One thing had become clear through all of this: Football life at the Capstone certainly was not dull.

**Opposite:** Alabama's teams always carried the hallmark of spirited defensive play, as demonstrated by Roman Harper (41), Todd Bates (56), Derrick Pope (6), and Chris James in surrounding a Tennessee running back.

**Left:** Alabama's Tyler Watts is smiling all the way into the end zone as he scores a touchdown against Tennessee during the Tide's 34-14 victory in 2002.

**Above:** Nothing succeeds like success, as Alabama's players demonstrate after their 34-14 win against Tennessee. The victory was part of a five-game winning streak that eventually brought Alabama a 10-3 record in 2002 under coach Dennis Franchione.

# 9

# HECTIC TIMES

labama football had never seen such hectic times as occurred after the 2002 season, and indeed for several seasons thereafter. Soon after head coach Dennis Franchione's abbreviated two-year term had ended, Mike Price was hired as his successor, but he never even coached a game. Off-the-field conduct caused him to resign just three months before practice was due to begin for the 2003 season.

Help was quickly and desperately needed, so the Tide turned to one of its playing heroes from the eighties, Mike Shula, a quarterback under Ray Perkins during the 1984-86 seasons. He was still warmly remembered at the Capstone as a gutsy and resourceful quarterback who compensated for a lack of great physical skills with a keen and instinctive mind and a never-say-die attitude on the playing field. His record as a starter during those seasons was 24-11-1, including victories in the Aloha and Sun Bowls and unforgettable last-minute comeback wins against Georgia and archrival Auburn in 1985.

He had played just one season in the NFL, with Tampa Bay, then followed the coaching footsteps of his father, Pro Football Hall of Fame

**Right: When Mike Shula (left) became Alabama's head coach in 2003, his quarterback was Brodie Croyle (right), who ultimately became the school's all-time leader in attempts (869), completions (488), yards (6,382), and TD passes (41).**

**Opposite: Mike Shula had little time to prepare for his first season as head coach in 2003, but still got off to a good start by winning his first game against South Florida, 40-17. That good fortune was short-lived as the Tide finished 4-9 with six of the losses by a touchdown or less, including two in overtime.**

coach Don Shula, for the next 15 years in the NFL as an assistant at Miami, Chicago, and Tampa Bay, where he was offensive coordinator. He was in his second tour with the Dolphins, as their quarterback coach, when the frantic call came from Alabama asking him to become its head coach. At age 38, he would be the second-youngest head coach in Division 1-A.

Shula, like his immediate predecessors, stepped into a morass created by NCAA sanctions. The continuity that is so important for a successful football program had disappeared. He was the fourth appointed head coach since Gene Stallings retired after the 1996 season, and the seventh since the immortal Bear Bryant stepped down just 20 years earlier.

His first season in 2003 produced a 4-9 record, but also included a lifetime of coaching experiences. Shula had only weeks, not months or years, to settle into the job and prepare a team about which he knew little. He had no spring practice during which he could introduce and try to perfect his system with a team that had been stripped by graduation losses and weakened by a substantial decline of new players because of the NCAA sanctions.

The schedule offered little help because the season's second game, after an opening 40-17 win against South Florida, was against top-ranked Oklahoma, and the Sooners laid bare, in winning 20-13, a preview of football life in the upcoming season. Alabama was always close, but the ability to overcome the Sooners was dogged by three lost fumbles, five sacks, and two interceptions. The bright spots were on defense, where linebackers Derrick Pope and Demeco Ryans accounted for 17 and 16 tackles, respectively.

That game became a mantra of sorts of the season because the Tide was 0-6 in games decided by one touchdown or less, including overtime losses to Arkansas and Tennessee, and a 28-23 loss to Auburn.

But of all the games in 2003, none ever will compare, in any era, to the record-setting 51-43 loss in five overtime periods to Tennessee at Bryant-Denny Stadium. The drama began after Casey Clausen's touchdown pass and an extra point for Tennessee with 25 seconds to play tied the score at 20-20. The Vols then blocked Brian Bostick's 45-yard field goal attempt with five seconds left to force the overtime.

**Left: Running back Shaud Williams displays his power running style that enabled him to lead the 2003 Tide with 1,367 rushing yards and 14 touchdowns.**

The teams matched touchdowns and extra points in the first two overtime periods and were tied 34-34. In the third period, both scored touchdowns but missed two-point conversions, upping the score to 40-40; both made field goals in the fourth period for a 43-43 tie; and

**Right: QB Brodie Croyle was fearless while standing in the pocket trying to pass as he showed against a fierce pass rush put on him by Ole Miss in 2003.**

Tennessee finally broke open the game in the fifth overtime period on Clausen's quarterback sneak and a two–point conversion. Alabama could not make a first down in four plays, though Tyrone Prothro had gained nine yards on the Tide's first play. They lost two yards on the next two plays and Croyle's fourth down pass to Fulgham was incomplete. Tennessee won the game, 51-43.

During the five overtimes, the teams ran 45 plays. This drama capped a game in which there was a total of 965 yards, 492-473 in favor of Tennessee. Alabama's Shaud Williams led all rushers with 166 yards while Croyle completed 21 of 38 passes for 215 yards.

**Left: Running back Shaud Williams in action against the University of Hawaii in 2003.**

**Above: Shaud Williams attacks Auburn's defense in 2003. In the 2002-03 seasons, he averaged 5.6 yards per carry, second best in Alabama history for a running back with 400 or more rushing attempts.**

The battle-hardening that the Tide players underwent in 2003 began to pay off with three victories to start the 2004 season. But the football gods stopped smiling when Alabama was ahead 31-0 against Western Carolina in the third game and Croyle, whose 488 pass completions and 6,382 passing yards rank first in Alabama history, tore up his right knee. He was finished

for the season, an irreplaceable loss for Alabama, and in short order the season-ending injury list soon included tailback Ray Hudson and starting fullback Tim Castille. Shula struggled to find starters, but despite a succession of gritty performances, Alabama won just three of its last eight games to finish 6-5 in the regular season. The Tide was invited to the Music City Bowl, its first post-season game in three years, but it could not match nor stop Minnesota's running game and lost 20-16 for a 6-6 overall record.

It appeared that Shula had achieved an amazing turnaround in 2005 when Alabama won its first nine games and raced to a fourth-place national ranking, despite losing star wide receiver Tyrone Prothro. His major ingredients were the passing of Croyle (2,499 yards, 14 touchdown passes, and only four interceptions); the rushing of Ken Darby (1,242 yards for a 103.5 per game average); receivers D.J. Hall (48-676, 5 touchdowns) and Keith Brown (34-642, 4 touchdowns) while picking up for Prothro; kicker Jamie Christensen whose field goals in the final seconds accounted for the winning points against Mississippi, Tennessee, and a 13-10 victory over Texas Tech in the Cotton Bowl; and a great defense that, during a mid-season run, did not allow a touchdown in four of five games, including a memorable 6-3 victory over Tennessee. The teams played a scoreless first half, but two field goals by Christensen, the last with 12 seconds to play, got the win. Consecutive season-ending losses to LSU and Auburn took the Tide out of the national championship race, but helped by their Cotton Bowl victory, Alabama still managed an eighth-place national ranking.

The magic of the 10-win season in 2005 disappeared in 2006, though Alabama got off to a 3-0 start and won five of its first seven games. But consecutive losses to Arkansas, in overtime, and Florida during that time had derailed the Tide and the wheels finally came off as they lost four of their last five games. One loss was to Tennessee, after leading for more than 50 minutes; another was to archrival Auburn.

Shula was fired a week after losing to Auburn, despite having signed a multi-million dollar contract extension in 2005 that was to keep him as head coach until 2012. He disagreed with the school's decision to remove him, citing the fact that from the start, he had to endure "inherited restrictions, including probation and scholarship limits," and maintained that his team's 10-2 record the previous year was "no fluke . . . but evidence of a program on the rise."

**Left: Running back Ken Darby took over the rushing chores for Alabama in 2004 and became a workhorse. He had 36 carries in a game against Mississippi and 35 against LSU, both among the top ten figures in the school's history.**

**Opposite: Ken Darby continued the long Alabama tradition of successful, big yardage-gaining running backs during the 2004-06 seasons.**

Right: Alabama receivers were expected to do more than just catch passes. Flanker Keith Brown carries the ball on an end around play in a 2005 game against South Carolina while helping the Tide to a 37-14 victory.

Far right: Running back D.J. Hall in action for the Tide against Florida during the 2006 season.

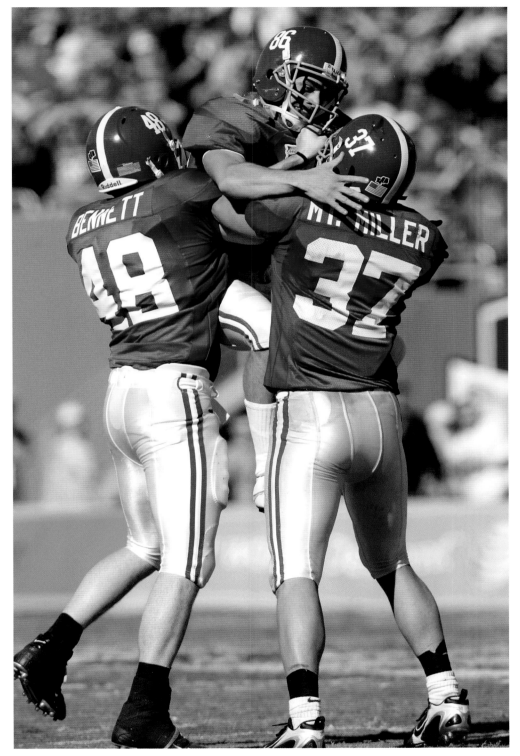

For the next month, Tide fans played another set of "who's the coach?" and at every turn, the name Nick Saban, then leading the NFL's Miami Dolphins, seemed to emerge. He had 11 years of college head coaching experience at Toledo, Michigan State, and LSU, during which time he amassed a record of 91-42-1. He was well known to Alabama fans from his successful five-season career (2000-2004) at Louisiana State, which included winning the national championship in 2003. His teams also beat Alabama four out of five years.

After a month of denials and evasions while the Dolphins still were playing, Saban finally accepted the job to become Alabama's 27th coach on January 3, 2007. His coming to the Capstone drove expectations to giddy heights when more than 92,000 Tide fans showed up for the annual "A Day" spring scrimmage.

Fans saw that as a great start for a new chapter of Alabama football history.

**Left: Alabama kicker Jamie Christensen (86) celebrates with teammates Kyle Bennett (48) and Matt Miller (37) after kicking the game-winning field goal that gave Alabama a 13-10 victory over Texas Tech in the 2006 Cotton Bowl.**

**Above: Christensen's field goal in the 2006 Cotton Bowl was one of three game-winners that he kicked during the season. His other kicks brought victories over Mississippi and Tennessee.**

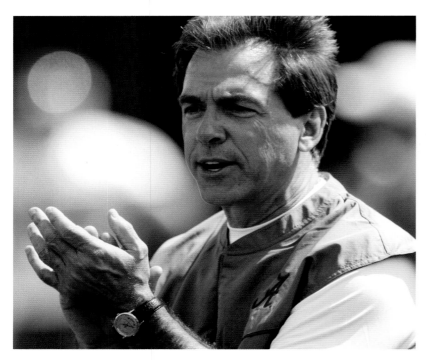

**Above:** Nick Saban was chosen to lead the Alabama football program as it began the 2007 season. He had been a successful college coach in three previous jobs at Toledo, Michigan State, and LSU and came to Alabama after coaching the Miami Dolphins.

**Right:** Mark Anderson (47) and DeMeco Ryans (35) sack Texas Tech's quarterback in the 2006 Cotton Bowl. Defense was a hallmark of that team because it did not allow opponents to score a touchdown in four of five games during a mid-season winning streak.

**Opposite:** Alabama raises the Cotton Bowl Trophy in celebration of its 2006 victory. It was the third time in its football history that Alabama came away with a Cotton Bowl victory.

# 10

# THE TIDE vs. THE TIGER

The soul of college football is found in the many rivalries that make up its continuing history. To Alabamans, none is more vibrant than the intra-state rivalry they call the Iron Bowl, the annual battle between Alabama and Auburn.

The weekly magazine *Sports Illustrated* once called Alabama versus Auburn "the best rivalry in the land, bar none, for the year-round passion it generates in Dixie. This rivalry is so heated that a local TV station decided not to interrupt the 2000 Iron Bowl for the result of the presidential recount announcement."

Some of the greatest stars from each school, such as the Tide's Bobby Marlow, Pat Trammell, Joe Namath, Ken Stabler, Tony Nathan, and Shaun Alexander, and Auburn's Pat Sullivan, Terry Beasley, Tucker Frederickson, Joe Cribbs, and Bo Jackson have etched their exploits on this series. There would have been more had there not been a 41-year interruption that began in 1908 when the schools severed football relations over petty disputes involving selection of the umpire for that year's game and the amount of per diem that should be paid to the players.

Consequently, as storied college football rivalries are ranked, this is a relative newcomer in the number of games played. Of course, controversy was part of the scene even before the first game was played

on February 22, 1893, when the teams disputed whether that game was part of the 1892 season (Alabama) or the first game of the 1893 season (Auburn). The matter was finally resolved in Alabama's favor many years later.

On the day of the first game, some 2,000 people came from all parts of the state for the 3:30 P.M. kickoff at Birmingham's Lakeview Park, where the Tide had played three earlier games during its first season. Alabama's coach was Eli Abbott, who was also its best player, and he dressed his team in solid white uniforms, with red stockings and a large red "U of A" adorning their sweaters.

Auburn, which also had started its football program in 1892, won the first coin toss and chose to receive the kickoff. Who returned that kickoff still is unknown, but Auburn's J.C. Dunham gained ten yards on the first scrimmage play.

The game, won by Auburn 32-22, actually was one of the most interesting in the history of the series. It was tightly contested as both teams displayed plenty of offense. Alabama touchdowns by Frank Savage and D.H. Smith kept the Tide within two points at halftime. Team captain W.G. Little ran 35 yards in the second half for a third touchdown. The Tide trailed by just two points midway through the second half until Auburn's team captain, Tom Daniels, broke open the game with two touchdowns and two extra points.

**Opposite: It is a battle for "bragging rights" for the state of Alabama each year when the Crimson Tide plays Auburn. In many years, the SEC title also has been at stake.**

After the game, Delma Wilson, one of Birmingham's "loveliest," presented Daniels with a special cup that still sits in a trophy case in Auburn's athletic center. The following day, the *Birmingham News* opined that it was "the greatest football game ever played in the state of Alabama."

Nine months later, the teams were paid $350 each to play in Montgomery, and Auburn won that second game, 40-16. Alabama's biggest moment was a 45-yard touchdown run by Dave Grayson. The Tide finally beat Auburn 18-0 in 1894, but defeated the Tigers just three more times, in 1903 and in 1905-06, and played a 6-6 tie in 1907, before the lights went out until 1948.

The biggest loss from the interruption was the lack of opportunities for each school's great teams during most of the first half of the twentieth century to play each other, thus negating the important "bragging rights" that really are the big prize between fierce rivals.

Opposite left: Clem Welch (top), Ed Salem (middle), and Gordon Pettus (bottom) score TDs in Alabama's rousing 55-0 victory, which renewed the rivalry against Auburn in 1948.

Opposite right: Legion Field in Birmingham, where the Alabama-Auburn game was always played until 1989.

Left: Quarterback Pat Trammell (12) helped Bear Bryant to his first victory over Auburn as Alabama's head coach in 1959.

**Opposite:** QB Joe Namath (12) and wide receiver Ray Perkins (88) teamed up on a 23-yard touchdown play for the winning points in a 21-14 victory over Auburn in 1964, clinching the national championship.

**Left:** Although he started just one game in three seasons against Auburn, quarterback Steadman Shealy rang up 26 points. In 1979, he ran for the winning touchdown in a 25-18 victory, which secured the national title for the Tide.

**Above:** Alabama's Johnny Musso (22) evades Auburn tacklers en route to a 31-7 Tide victory in 1971.

Coach Bear Bryant always lamented the fact that the two schools had not competed when he played at Alabama. "I missed out on some of the tradition of the series," he noted while head coach at Alabama. "But I can assure you that as a coach, it made me work harder."

The state's legislature finally intervened in 1947 and directed that the boards of trustees from both schools get together and restart the rivalry "no later than May 1949." Eight months later, peace was achieved, and the rivalry has sizzled ever since it was resumed on December 4, 1948, at Birmingham's Legion Field. Alabama won that renewal game 55-0 as Ed Salem threw three touchdown passes, ran for another score, and kicked six extra points. Marlow became the series' first player to score three touchdowns in one game, and he did it twice in Alabama's decisive victories in the 1950-51 games.

**Below: Bear Bryant's players celebrate his tying Amos Alonzo Stagg's all-time 314-victory mark in 1981 after a win at Penn State. He established a new mark the following week with a 28-17 victory over archrival Auburn.**

**Right: Ironically, after Bear Bryant's teams had beaten Auburn nine times in a row, from 1973-81, the Tigers defeated his last Alabama team 23-22 in 1982, the final game that he coached in this historic rivalry.**

**Opposite: Van Tiffin kicked the final play, game-winning field goals in 1984 and 1985 against Auburn.**

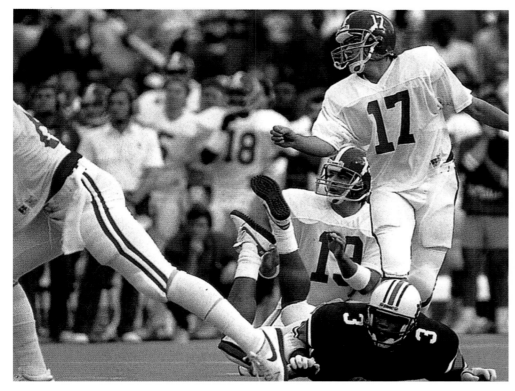

Alabama's early dominance in the series' resumption came to an abrupt halt when Shug Jordan became Auburn's head coach in 1951 and the Tide was defeated in four consecutive years, one of those wins capping the Tigers' national championship in 1957.

Bryant's coming to Alabama in 1958 keyed the onset of an overwhelming dominance by the Tide, which won nine of the first eleven games he coached against Auburn, including four straight shutouts from 1959-62. Overall, Bryant had a 19-6 record in the series. His most dramatic victory was on November 28, 1981, when he achieved career win No. 315, the most ever at that time by any college football coach. It wasn't easy because the Tide had to come from behind in the fourth quarter to defeat its most intense rival, 28-17.

Bryant got his first victory against Auburn in 1959 as Alabama's quarterback tandem of Trammell and Bobby Shelton combined for a 10-0 victory when Martin Dyess caught a late, 10-yard scoring pass from Shelton. In 1960,

**Opposite: The Tide won back Alabama bragging rights with a 16-7 victory over the Tigers in 1990.**

**Above: Alabama had scored in 30 consecutive games against Auburn until the Tide lost 10-0 in 1987.**

**Right: QB Gary Hollingsworth, who had already thrown a TD pass, evades Auburn's pass rush in the 1989 game. Auburn's strong defense denied Alabama its first-place ranking and an undisputed SEC title as the Tide fell 30-20.**

Alabama's top-ranked defense, led by linebacker Leroy Jordan, was abetted by Trammell's 13-yard pass to Bill Battle, setting up Tommy Brooker's winning 13-yard field goal in a 3-0 victory. A year later, Trammell and Battle again made a host of big plays as Alabama clinched an unbeaten season and the national championship with a 34-0 win.

Two of Alabama's biggest quarterback stars, Joe Namath and Ken Stabler, left their marks on the series. As a sophomore in 1962, Namath threw two touchdown passes and scored a third in Alabama's 38-0 victory, while two years later, he capped his career and Alabama's national championship with a clinching 23-yard touchdown pass to end Ray Perkins in a 21-14 victory. In addition to Namath's passing that day, the Tide got a huge boost from Ray Ogden's 107-yard kickoff return, which opened the second half and overcame a 7-6 halftime deficit. Stabler, never known for his running skills, made the key play in the

Opposite: Total intensity was the name of the game whenever Alabama and Auburn played each other Particularly on defense. Here the Tide stacks a first down sneak attempt by Auburn's quarterback in the 1994 game.

Left: Alabama defensive back Sam Shade is welcomed by his teammates after coming up with a big defensive play against Auburn in the 1994 game.

**Right: Santonio Beard caps a 100-yard offensive day with a touchdown in Alabama's 31-7 victory over Auburn in 2001.**

**Opposite: Alabama players hoist the Iron Bowl Trophy during an on-campus celebration after defeating archrival Auburn 31-7 in 2001.**

Tide's 7-3 victory in 1967 when he slogged 47 yards for the game's only touchdown over a rain-soaked field.

The 1969 game was a shootout and Auburn won, 49-26. But Alabama quarterback Scott Hunter set a series passing record that still stands—30 completions for 484 yards. David Bailey caught nine of those passes, also a series record that still exists.

Running back Johnny Musso established himself as one of the most outstanding performers in this series in the 1970-71 games. Although Auburn won another wild-and-wooly affair 33-28 in 1970, Musso ran for 221 yards, still the second most rushing yards in one game behind Morrow's 1951 total of 233 yards. The following year, Musso arrived at the stadium on crutches because of an injured big toe, but in the game, he exploded on 31 runs for 167 yards to help Alabama win, 31-7.

Alabama blew a 16-3 lead and lost 17-16 in 1972, and that was the last time a Bryant-coached team ever lost to Auburn. The Tide reeled off nine straight wins, the series' longest winning streak by either team, with an average victory margin of 16.5 points, and shutting out Auburn four times in those games.

In the late 70s, quarterbacks Jeff Rutledge and Steadman Shealy had some of their best days against Auburn. Rutledge, who threw six touchdown passes in his three games against Auburn, got three in a 34-16 victory in 1978. Shealy, his understudy during two of those seasons, scored 26 points in three games. He passed for one touchdown and ran for two, including the game-winner, in a 25-18 victory in 1979, preserving Alabama's first unbeaten regular season since 1974.

Life for Alabama against Auburn after Bryant's departure often was very iffy. The Tide sandwiched a pair of two-point victories, decided by Van Tiffin's final-play field goals in 1984-85, between a three and four-point loss in 1983 and 1986. In 1990, Gene Stallings became the first coach since Harold (Red) Drew in 1948, to beat Auburn in his first season—even Bryant lost his first game, 14-8 in 1958. Dennis Franchione also duplicated Stallings's feat in 2001 with a 31-7 victory.

After the series restarted in 1948, the teams always played each other at Legion Field in Birmingham, considered a "neutral" site. Auburn broke that tradition in 1989 and moved its home game against the Tide to its Jordan-Hare Stadium where it won for a fourth straight time, 30-20. The Tigers also capped a perfect season at home in 1993 when their 22-14 victory was keyed by James Bostic's 70-yard run with just over two minutes to play.

It wasn't until 1999 that Alabama finally got a victory at Auburn, winning 28-17 while also clinching the SEC's Western Division title. Shaun Alexander ripped off over 100 rushing yards in the final quarter and

added three touchdowns for the Tide. Alabama, led by Andrew Zow's passing and 100 rushing yards each by Andrew Galloway and Santonio Beard, made it two wins in a row at Jordan-Hare Stadium in 2001 with a 31-7 victory, the Tide's most lopsided victory over Auburn since 1977.

Alabama continued to use Legion Field for its home games against Auburn until 2000 when the Tide also "went home" to Bryant-Denny Stadium in Tuscaloosa. Since that time, the home games have alternated between the two campus sites, and Auburn has won six of the seven games since the change.

But the beat goes on in the Iron Bowl, where all of Alabama has a vested interest in which team gets the all-important annual braggin' rights as to whose fans can legitimately say "We're Number 1!"

# 11

# BOWLIN' WITH 'BAMA

**P**ost-season bowl games are synonymous with Alabama football. And why not?

Starting back in 1926 when it defeated the University of Washington in the Rose Bowl, the Tide has played more than 50 games in 15 post-season bowls, more than any college team in the nation. During an 80-year stretch since that time, there have been only 26 years when an Alabama team was not invited or did not earn the right to play in a bowl game; in the last half of the twentieth century, there was an Alabama team playing in 40 of the 50 bowl seasons.

In cold numbers, Alabama once appeared in 25 straight bowls—unmatched by any school in history—from 1959 through 1983. In 24 of those years, Bear Bryant was the team's head coach. The only year he missed bringing a team to post-season play during his 25-year coaching tenure at Alabama was in 1958, his first year at the Capstone when he was rebuilding the school's football program.

Until 1988, when the Bowl Championship Series began, a bowl invitation was always the reward for having a fine season, be it in terms of season victories or when conference titles earned bowl trips. That is why Alabama has played in a dozen Sugar Bowls; as the winner of its Southeastern Conference it was the host team. The Sugar Bowl now is part of the current BCS as a means of deciding the national champion.

In recent years, the proliferation of bowl games has dulled the luster of post-season play, to the point that there are enough bowl games to accommodate more than half the college teams in the NCAA's Division 1-A level of football-playing schools.

This in no way diminishes Alabama's proud bowl history. Its teams have participated because their excellence earned the invitations. Their fans have been an equally important factor, offering tremendous support by traveling in huge numbers to the bowl sites, where their economic impact has always been significant.

**Opposite above: Alabama's rich bowl history began with five appearances in the Rose Bowl. Here the unbeaten 1937 team limbers up a few days before playing California in the 1938 game where it suffered its first postseason loss, 13-0.**

**Opposite bottom: Alabama came from behind to beat Boston College 37-21 in the 1943 Orange Bowl. BC's Mike Holovak muffs a pass as a Tide defender closes in.**

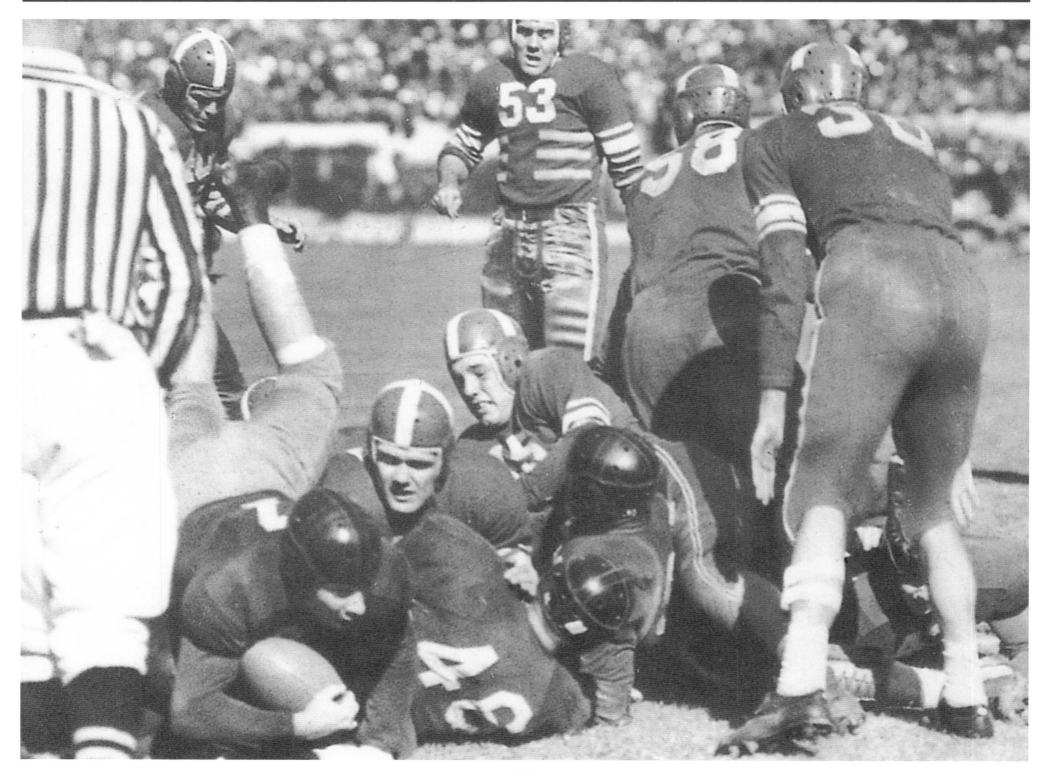

Opposite: Norwood Hodges scores against Duke in the 1945 Sugar Bowl.

Left: In their final trip to the Rose Bowl, in 1946, the Tide defeated Southern Cal 34-14. Harry Gilmer, at the bottom of this pile after a one-yard TD plunge, also passed for a touchdown, one of three that he threw in post-season games.

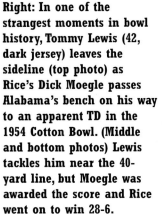

**Opposite: Alabama's Bob Conway returns a kickoff following Syracuse's only touchdown in the Tide's 61-6 romp in the 1953 Orange Bowl.**

**Right: In one of the strangest moments in bowl history, Tommy Lewis (42, dark jersey) leaves the sideline (top photo) as Rice's Dick Moegle passes Alabama's bench on his way to an apparent TD in the 1954 Cotton Bowl. (Middle and bottom photos) Lewis tackles him near the 40-yard line, but Moegle was awarded the score and Rice went on to win 28-6.**

**Far right: Quarterback Joe Namath, a sophomore, scampers for a few yards during Alabama's 13-0 victory against Oklahoma in the 1963 Orange Bowl.**

Alabama started its post-season heritage as a five-time Rose Bowl participant between 1926 and 1938. Until the Orange Bowl began in 1933, the Rose Bowl—"the granddaddy of all bowls"—was the only post-season bowl game available, and being invited as a participant was the singular post-season honor. It began as a one-year event, a part of the 1902 Tournament of Roses Festival in Pasadena where Michigan defeated Stanford, 49-0. The event's organizers abandoned football after just one game and turned to a variety of events such as Roman chariot racing, tug-of-war matches, track and field events, and polo matches before eventually reviving the football game on an annual basis—the Rose Bowl—in 1916.

Ten years later, the committee invited Wallace Wade's Alabama team to play the University of Washington in the 1926 game. In subsequent years, five of Wade's teams from Alabama and Duke were invited.

Wade, and later Frank Thomas, coached every Alabama team that played in the Rose Bowl. The Tide notched three victories and a tie in its first four Rose Bowl appearances, and has an overall 4-1-1 record as the event's most frequent participant from outside of the Pac-10 and Big 10.

In 1926, running back Johnny Mack Brown scored two touchdowns on passes from Pooley Hubert and Grant Gillis during an eight-minute, 20-point surge in the third quarter that brought the Tide from a 12-0 halftime deficit to a 20-19 victory. "Pooley told me to run as fast as I could toward the end zone. When I reached the three-yard line, I looked up for the ball and it was coming down over my shoulder. I took it in stride, stiff-armed one tackler and carried another over the goal line with me," Brown said of his second touchdown. The following year Alabama, though out-gained 305-98, tied Stanford 7-7.

In Wade's final game as Alabama's coach in the 1931 Rose Bowl, he stunned everyone by starting his "shock troops," comprised mostly of substitutes, to soften up Washington State's unbeaten "Wonder Team."

It must have worked because the Tide scored 21 points in the second quarter en route to a 24-0 victory.

Thomas was head coach in 1935 when the famed trio of Dixie Howell, Don Hutson, and Bear Bryant combined to give the Tide a 22-7 halftime lead. Howell scored two rushing touchdowns, one of 67 yards, and completed seven passes to Bryant and Hutson culminating in a 29-13 victory.

The Tide unaccountably turned over the ball eight times in the 1938 Rose Bowl, paving the way for a 13-0 victory by Southern California.

In 1946, the last year before the Rose Bowl signed a pact to feature only the winners of the Pacific Coast Conference (later Pac-8 and Pac-10) and the Big Ten, Alabama defeated Southern California 34-14. The Tide's defense held USC to just 41 total yards of offense while All-America

Opposite: Joe Namath, playing on a injured leg, completed 18 of 37 for 255 yards and two TDs in the 1965 Orange Bowl against Texas.

Left: Tim Davis kicks the first of four field goals in Alabama's 12-7 win over Ole Miss in the 1964 Sugar Bowl.

running back Harry Gilmer led Alabama with 116 rushing yards and a touchdown pass.

The post-season bowls have also played a major role in Alabama's national championships. It wasn't until 1965 that post-season results had any bearing on poll rankings. That season the fourth-ranked Tide played No. 3 Nebraska in the Orange Bowl's first night game. During the afternoon, top-ranked Michigan State had lost to UCLA and second-ranked Arkansas was defeated by LSU. Alabama's players were told before they went on the field that they had a chance to win the national championship.

Alabama quarterback Steve Sloan's instructions for the game were to "throw the ball any time you want," and Sloan completed a pair of touchdown passes to Ray Perkins among his 296 passing yards as Alabama won, 39-28. The following year, Alabama beat Nebraska 34-7 in the Sugar Bowl but finished third in the final polls.

Bryant's 1973, 1978, and 1979 teams clinched their national championships as the host team in the Sugar Bowl. So did Gene Stallings's 1992 team, the only national champions of the post-Bryant era.

In 1973, Alabama, top-ranked before the game, lost to Notre Dame. Trailing 24-23, the Tide had the Irish backed up to their two-yard line in the final minutes and needed only to stop them on third down to get the ball for what they were sure would be a game-winning drive. Notre Dame quarterback Tom Clements fooled Alabama's defense which were expecting a running play to give the Irish punter more room to kick on fourth down. Instead, he passed 35 yards to tight end Robin Weber to let Notre Dame keep the ball and foil any comeback dramas. Though Alabama lost, it still split the national championship with Notre Dame.

The Tide defeated Penn State 14-7 in 1979, as Major Ogilvie's eight-yard touchdown run in the third quarter broke a 7-7 tie. The defense won the game with a pair of goal line stands in the fourth quarter. Linebacker Barry Krauss stopped Penn State's Mike Guman on fourth down at the goal line to preserve the victory.

Alabama repeated as national champion the following year with a 24-9 victory over Arkansas. In its fifth straight bowl victory, four of them in the Sugar Bowl, Ogilvie and Alabama's defense were the principal forces. In the first half, Ogilvie scored two touchdowns and set up a field goal to help the Tide to a 17-3 lead. After Arkansas closed to 17-9, quarterback Steadman Shealy engineered a magnificent 98-yard drive, capped by Steve Whitman's 12-yard touchdown run.

**Left: Alabama's offense lines up at midfield in the 1979 Sugar Bowl against Penn State. It took a pair of legendary goal line stands in the fourth quarter by the Tide's defense to nail down the 14-7 victory and so it became known as "the goal line stand game."**

**Right:** Alabama defense celebrates after recovering a turnover that helped to clinch a 24-9 victory over Arkansas in the 1980 Sugar Bowl.

**Opposite above:** Quarterback David Smith was Alabama's chief offensive weapon against Army's deadly wishbone offense and he completed 33 of 43 passes for 412 yards as the Tide eked out a 29-28 victory.

**Opposite below:** Defensive back George Teague high-steps his way into the end zone with one of two interceptions that Alabama's defense turned into second-half touchdowns in its 34-23 victory over Miami in the 1993 Sugar Bowl.

Alabama's surprising 34-23 romp over the University of Miami in the 1993 game propelled the Tide to an undefeated season and the national championship. At the time, the Hurricanes were ranked No. 1 and Alabama was No. 2, but Tide coach Gene Stallings was not deterred. Stallings was confident that his top-ranked rushing defense could handle Miami's running game. Alabama limited the Hurricanes to just 48 yards on the ground. With Alabama ahead 13-6 at halftime, a pair of interceptions that led to two touchdowns within 16 seconds in the third quarter crushed any comeback hopes by Miami.

The Liberty Bowl, which didn't begin until 1959, has a special place in Alabama's football history. The Tide was invited to play in the bowl's first game, then held in Philadelphia, against Penn State. Though Alabama lost 7-0, it was the first big step in Bryant's reclamation of Alabama's football program that went on to include 23 more post-season games during the rest of his career at the Capstone. The 1982 Liberty Bowl, then played in Memphis, was also his final game as Alabama's head coach. Bryant's team defeated Illinois

21-15 as defensive back Jeremiah Castille intercepted three Illini passes, the last one ending a potential game-winning drive.

In the history of the bowls Alabama has seen many other individual post-season highlights. For instance, Alabama made its first Cotton Bowl appearance in 1942 against Texas A&M and was totally ineffective with just one first down, one pass completion, and 75 rushing yards. But they transformed a dozen turnovers into 29 points for a 29-21 victory. In 1963, quarterback Joe Namath helped Alabama to a 17-0 victory over Oklahoma in the Orange Bowl. Two years later, hampered by a knee injury so painful that he was unable to start the Sugar Bowl, Namath completed 18 of 37 passes for 255 yards and two touchdowns and was chosen the game's most valuable player. Alabama lost the game, but it took a mighty tackle by Texas linebacker Tommy Nobis to stop Namath at the goal line as he tried to score the winning points. In 1988, David Smith completed 33 of 43 passes against Army in the Sun Bowl for 412 yards, tops in Tide history. Marco Battle and Greg Payne each caught a record nine passes. In 1995, running back Sherman Williams had arguably the greatest offensive day by any Alabama player in a bowl game when he gained a record 359 yards (161 rushing yards, 155 from pass receptions, and 38 on kickoff returns) in the Citrus Bowl victory over Ohio State. In the 2006 Cotton Bowl against Texas Tech, Brodie Croyle's 76-yard touchdown pass to Keith Brown was

Opposite: Alabama's players celebrate their dominating 34-23 victory over Miami in the 1993 Sugar Bowl, having clinched the only national championship the Tide had notched since the end of the Bear Bryant era.

Above: No one enjoys Alabama's bowl games more than its fans, shown parading down New Orleans' Bourbon Street before the 1990 Sugar Bowl.

Right: Gene Stallings, flanked by two of his players, led the Tide to a berth in the Fiesta Bowl in his first season as head coach.

**Opposite Left: Running back Sherman Williams had one of the greatest offensive days by an Alabama player during the 1995 Citrus Bowl against Ohio State when he amassed 359 total yards—161 by rushing, 151 by pass receiving, and 38 on kickoff returns.**

**Opposite Right: Alabama head coach Gene Stallings had a 5-1 record in post-season play during his seven-season tenure.**

**Right: Terry Jones, Jr. (82) catches a touchdown pass against Iowa State during Alabama's 14-13 victory in the 2001 Independence Bowl.**

**Below: Quarterback Brodie Croyle is congratulated by head coach Mike Shula after Miami's 13-10 win over Texas Tech in the 2006 Cotton Bowl. Croyle's school record 76-yard touchdown pass to Keith Brown was the margin of victory.**

the longest in Alabama bowl history and part of a record-setting 141 receiving yards game.

But the most unforgettable play in college bowl history still belongs to Alabama halfback Tommy Lewis in the 1954 Cotton Bowl when he jumped off the bench and tackled Rice's Dick Moegle who was running down the sideline, ostensibly en route to a touchdown. Lewis ran onto the field, sending Moegle to the ground with a shoulder tackle; just as quickly, he trotted off the field and back to the bench. Referee Cliff Shaw witnessed the entire action and he awarded Moegle a 95-yard touchdown.

Crushed at his precipitous and obviously illegal act, Lewis went to Rice's locker room at halftime to apologize to coach Jess Neely. Neely saw Lewis's obvious distress and simply consoled him. "Don't let it bother you," he told the player.

Lewis said after the game: "I'm too emotional. I kept telling myself, 'I didn't do it. I didn't do it.' But I knew I had. I'm just too full of Alabama. He just ran too close. I know I'll hear about it for the rest of my life."

# ALABAMA CRIMSON TIDE FOOTBALL RECORDS

## YEAR-BY-YEAR RESULTS

| Year | Coach | W | L | T | Pts | Opp | Year | Coach | W | L | T | Pts | Opp |
|------|-------|---|---|---|-----|-----|------|-------|---|---|---|-----|-----|
| 1892 | E. N. Beaumont | 2 | 2 | 0 | 96 | 37 | 1950 | H. D. Drew | 9 | 2 | 0 | 328 | 107 |
| 1893 | Eli Abbott | 0 | 4 | 0 | 24 | 74 | 1951 | H. D. Drew | 5 | 6 | 0 | 263 | 188 |
| 1894 | Eli Abbott | 3 | 1 | 0 | 60 | 16 | 1952 | H. D. Drew | 10 | 2 | 0 | 325 | 139 |
| 1895 | Eli Abbott | 0 | 4 | 0 | 12 | 112 | 1953 | H. D. Drew | 6 | 3 | 3 | 178 | 152 |
| 1896 | Otto Wagonhurst | 2 | 1 | 0 | 56 | 10 | 1954 | H. D. Drew | 4 | 5 | 2 | 123 | 104 |
| 1897 | Allen McCants | 1 | 0 | 0 | 6 | 0 | 1955 | J. B. Whitworth | 0 | 10 | 0 | 48 | 256 |
| 1898 | No Team | | | | | | 1956 | J. B. Whitworth | 2 | 7 | 1 | 85 | 208 |
| 1899 | W. A Hartin | 3 | 1 | 0 | 39 | 31 | 1957 | J. B. Whitworth | 2 | 7 | 1 | 69 | 173 |
| 1900 | M. Griffin | 2 | 3 | 0 | 52 | 99 | 1958 | Paul W. Bryant | 5 | 4 | 1 | 106 | 75 |
| 1901 | M. H. Harvey | 2 | 1 | 2 | 92 | 23 | 1959 | Paul W. Bryant | 7 | 2 | 2 | 95 | 59 |
| 1902 | Eli Abbott, J. O. Heyworth | 4 | 4 | 0 | 191 | 49 | 1960 | Paul W. Bryant | 8 | 1 | 2 | 183 | 56 |
| 1903 | W. B. Blount | 3 | 4 | 0 | 60 | 114 | 1961 | Paul W. Bryant | 11 | 0 | 0 | 297 | 25 |
| 1904 | W. B. Blount | 7 | 3 | 0 | 100 | 62 | 1962 | Paul W. Bryant | 10 | 1 | 0 | 289 | 39 |
| 1905 | Jack Leavenworth | 6 | 4 | 0 | 178 | 113 | 1963 | Paul W. Bryant | 9 | 2 | 0 | 227 | 95 |
| 1906 | J. W. H. Pollard | 5 | 1 | 0 | 97 | 82 | 1964 | Paul W. Bryant | 10 | 1 | 0 | 250 | 88 |
| 1907 | J. W. H. Pollard | 5 | 1 | 2 | 70 | 64 | 1965 | Paul W. Bryant | 9 | 1 | 1 | 256 | 107 |
| 1908 | J. W. H. Pollard | 6 | 1 | 1 | 108 | 31 | 1966 | Paul W. Bryant | 11 | 0 | 0 | 301 | 44 |
| 1909 | J. W. H. Pollard | 5 | 1 | 2 | 68 | 17 | 1967 | Paul W. Bryant | 8 | 2 | 1 | 204 | 131 |
| 1910 | Guy S. Lowman | 4 | 4 | 0 | 65 | 107 | 1968 | Paul W. Bryant | 8 | 3 | 0 | 184 | 139 |
| 1911 | D. V. Graves | 5 | 2 | 2 | 153 | 31 | 1969 | Paul W. Bryant | 6 | 5 | 0 | 314 | 268 |
| 1912 | D. V. Graves | 5 | 3 | 1 | 156 | 55 | 1970 | Paul W. Bryant | 6 | 5 | 1 | 334 | 264 |
| 1913 | D. V. Graves | 6 | 3 | 0 | 188 | 40 | 1971 | Paul W. Bryant | 11 | 1 | 0 | 368 | 122 |
| 1914 | D. V. Graves | 5 | 4 | 0 | 211 | 64 | 1972 | Paul W. Bryant | 10 | 2 | 0 | 406 | 150 |
| 1915 | Thomas Kelly | 6 | 2 | 0 | 250 | 51 | 1973 | Paul W. Bryant | 11 | 1 | 0 | 477 | 113 |
| 1916 | Thomas Kelly | 6 | 3 | 0 | 156 | 62 | 1974 | Paul W. Bryant | 11 | 1 | 0 | 329 | 96 |
| 1917 | Thomas Kelly | 5 | 2 | 1 | 168 | 29 | 1975 | Paul W. Bryant | 11 | 1 | 0 | 374 | 72 |
| 1918 | No Team | | | | | | 1976 | Paul W. Bryant | 9 | 3 | 0 | 327 | 140 |
| 1919 | Xen C. Scott | 8 | 1 | 0 | 280 | 22 | 1977 | Paul W. Bryant | 11 | 1 | 0 | 380 | 139 |
| 1920 | Xen C. Scott | 10 | 1 | 0 | 377 | 35 | 1978 | Paul W. Bryant | 11 | 1 | 0 | 345 | 168 |
| 1921 | Xen C. Scott | 5 | 4 | 2 | 241 | 104 | 1979 | Paul W. Bryant | 12 | 0 | 0 | 383 | 67 |
| 1922 | Xen C. Scott | 6 | 3 | 1 | 300 | 81 | 1980 | Paul W. Bryant | 10 | 2 | 0 | 352 | 98 |
| 1923 | Wallace Wade | 7 | 2 | 1 | 222 | 50 | 1981 | Paul W. Bryant | 9 | 2 | 1 | 296 | 151 |
| 1924 | Wallace Wade | 8 | 1 | 0 | 290 | 24 | 1982 | Paul W. Bryant | 8 | 4 | 0 | 317 | 201 |
| 1925 | Wallace Wade | 10 | 0 | 0 | 297 | 26 | 1983 | Ray Perkins | 8 | 4 | 0 | 366 | 229 |
| 1926 | Wallace Wade | 9 | 0 | 1 | 249 | 27 | 1984 | Ray Perkins | 5 | 6 | 0 | 226 | 208 |
| 1927 | Wallace Wade | 5 | 4 | 1 | 154 | 73 | 1985 | Ray Perkins | 9 | 2 | 1 | 318 | 181 |
| 1928 | Wallace Wade | 6 | 3 | 0 | 187 | 75 | 1986 | Ray Perkins | 10 | 3 | 0 | 351 | 163 |
| 1929 | Wallace Wade | 6 | 3 | 0 | 196 | 58 | 1987 | Bill Curry | 7 | 5 | 0 | 268 | 213 |
| 1930 | Wallace Wade | 10 | 0 | 0 | 271 | 13 | 1988 | Bill Curry | 9 | 3 | 0 | 317 | 188 |
| 1931 | Frank W. Thomas | 9 | 1 | 0 | 370 | 57 | 1989 | Bill Curry | 10 | 2 | 0 | 332 | 184 |
| 1932 | Frank W. Thomas | 8 | 2 | 0 | 200 | 51 | 1990 | Gene Stallings | 7 | 5 | 0 | 260 | 162 |
| 1933 | Frank W. Thomas | 7 | 1 | 1 | 130 | 17 | 1991 | Gene Stallings | 11 | 1 | 0 | 324 | 143 |
| 1934 | Frank W. Thomas | 10 | 0 | 0 | 316 | 45 | 1992 | Gene Stallings | 13 | 0 | 0 | 366 | 122 |
| 1935 | Frank W. Thomas | 6 | 2 | 1 | 185 | 55 | 1993* | Gene Stallings | 1 | 12 | 0 | 316 | 158 |
| 1936 | Frank W. Thomas | 8 | 0 | 1 | 168 | 35 | 1994 | Gene Stallings | 12 | 1 | 0 | 305 | 190 |
| 1937 | Frank W. Thomas | 9 | 1 | 0 | 225 | 33 | 1995 | Gene Stallings | 8 | 3 | 0 | 260 | 188 |
| 1938 | Frank W. Thomas | 7 | 1 | 1 | 149 | 40 | 1996 | Gene Stallings | 10 | 3 | 0 | 286 | 143 |
| 1939 | Frank W. Thomas | 5 | 3 | 1 | 101 | 53 | 1997 | Mike Dubose | 4 | 7 | 0 | 246 | 248 |
| 1940 | Frank W. Thomas | 7 | 2 | 0 | 166 | 80 | 1998 | Mike Dubose | 7 | 5 | 0 | 251 | 287 |
| 1941 | Frank W. Thomas | 9 | 2 | 0 | 263 | 85 | 1999 | Mike Dubose | 10 | 3 | 0 | 380 | 265 |
| 1942 | Frank W. Thomas | 8 | 3 | 0 | 246 | 97 | 2000 | Mike Dubose | 3 | 8 | 0 | 228 | 246 |
| 1943 | No Team | | | | | | 2001 | Dennis Franchione | 7 | 5 | 0 | 304 | 219 |
| 1944 | Frank W. Thomas | 5 | 2 | 2 | 272 | 83 | 2002 | Dennis Franchione | 10 | 3 | 0 | 367 | 200 |
| 1945 | Frank W. Thomas | 10 | 0 | 0 | 430 | 80 | 2003 | Mike Shula | 4 | 9 | 0 | 331 | 333 |
| 1946 | Frank W. Thomas | 7 | 4 | 0 | 186 | 110 | 2004 | Mike Shula | 6 | 6 | 0 | 295 | 189 |
| 1947 | H. D. Drew | 8 | 3 | 0 | 210 | 101 | 2005 | Mike Shula | 10 | 2 | 0 | 263 | 128 |
| 1948 | H. D. Drew | 6 | 4 | 1 | 228 | 170 | 2006 | Mike Shula | 6 | 7 | 0 | 301 | 247 |
| 1949 | H. D. Drew | 6 | 3 | 1 | 227 | 130 | | | | | | | |

*Original 9-3-1 record in 1993 changed by forfeits.

## TOP CAREER RUSHERS

| | Att. | Yds. | Avg. | TD |
|---|---|---|---|---|
| 1. Shaun Alexander (1996-99) | 727 | 3565 | 4.9 | 41 |
| 2. Bobby Humphrey (1985-88) | 615 | 3420 | 5.6 | 40 |
| 3. Johnny Musso (1969-71) | 574 | 2741 | 6.3 | 34 |
| 4. Dennis Riddle (1994-97) | 612 | 2645 | 4.3 | 12 |
| 5. Bobby Marlow (1950-52) | 408 | 2560 | 6.3 | 26 |

## TOP CAREER PASSERS

| | Att-Com | Pct. | Yds | TD |
|---|---|---|---|---|
| 1. Brodie Croyle (2002-05) | 869-488 | 56.2 | 6382 | 41 |
| 2. Andrew Zow (1998-2001) | 852-459 | 53.8 | 5983 | 35 |
| 3. Jay Barker (1991-94) | 706-4502 | 56.9 | 5689 | 26 |
| 4. Scott Hunter (1968-70) | 672-382 | 56.8 | 4899 | 27 |
| 5. Freddie Kitchens (1993-97) | 680-343 | 50.4 | 4668 | 30 |

## TOP CAREER RECEIVERS

| | Rec. | Yds. | Avg. | TD |
|---|---|---|---|---|
| 1. Freddie Milons (1998-01) | 152 | 1859 | 12.2 | 6 |
| 2. David Bailey (1969-71) | 132 | 1857 | 14.1 | 13 |
| 3. Lamonde Russell (1987-90) | 108 | 1332 | 12.3 | 5 |
| 4. Antonio Carter (1999-2001) | 106 | 1294 | 11.4 | 5 |
| 5. Curtis Brown (1991-95) | 106 | 1568 | 12.8 | 11 |

## TOP CAREER SCORERS

| | TD | FG | PAT | PTS |
|---|---|---|---|---|
| 1. Phillip Doyle (1987-90) | -- | 78 | 105 | 339 |
| 2. Michael Proctor (1992-95) | -- | 65 | 131 | 326 |
| 3. Van Tiffin (1983-86) | -- | 59 | 135 | 312 |
| 4. Shaun Alexander (1996-99) | 50 | -- | -- | 300 |
| 5. Bobby Humphrey (1985-88) | 40 | 2 | -- | 242 |

---

# BOWL RESULTS

**The Aloha Bowl – Honolulu, Hawaii**
Record: Won 1, Lost 0
1985 – Alabama 24, Southern Cal 3

**The Astro-Bluebonnet Bowl – Houston, Texas**
Record: Won 0, Lost 0, Tied 2
1960 – Alabama 3, Texas 3
1970 – Alabama 24, Oklahoma 24

**The Blockbuster Bowl – Miami, Florida**
Record: Won 1, Lost 0
1991 – Alabama 30, Colorado 25

**The Citrus Bowl – Orlando, Florida**
Record: Won 1, Lost 0
1995 – Alabama 24, Ohio State 17

**The Cotton Bowl – Dallas, Texas**
Record: Won 3, Lost 4
1942 – Alabama 29, Texas A&M 21
1954 – Rice 28, Alabama 6
1968 – Texas A&M 20, Alabama 16
1973 – Texas 17, Alabama 13
1981 – Alabama 30, Baylor 2
1982 – Texas 14, Alabama 12
2006 – Alabama 13, Texas Tech 10

**The Fiesta Bowl – Tempe, Arizona**
Record: Won 0, Lost 1
1991 – Louisville 35, Alabama 7

**The Gator Bowl – Jacksonville, Florida**
Record: Won 1, Lost 1
1968 – Missouri 35, Alabama 10
1993 – Alabama 24, North Carolina 10

**The Hall of Fame Bowl – Tampa, Florida**
Record: Won 0, Lost 1
1988 – Michigan 28, Alabama 24

**The Independence Bowl – Shreveport, Louisiana**
Record: Won 1, Lost 1
2001 – Alabama 14, Iowa State 13
2006 – Oklahoma State 34, Alabama 31

**The Liberty Bowl – Philadelphia & Memphis**
Record: Won 2, Lost 2
1959 – Penn State 7, Alabama 0
1969 – Colorado 47, Alabama 33
1976 – Alabama 36, UCLA 6
1982 – Alabama 21, Illinois 15

**The Music City Bowl – Nashville, Tennessee**
Record: Won 2, Lost 0
1998 – Virginia Tech 38, Alabama 7
2004 – Minnesota 20, Alabama 16

**The Orange Bowl – Miami, Florida**
Record: Won 4, Lost 4
1943 – Alabama 37, Boston College 21
1953 – Alabama 61, Syracuse 6
1963 – Alabama 17, Oklahoma 0
1965 – Texas 21, Alabama 17
1966 – Alabama 39, Nebraska 28
1972 – Nebraska 38, Alabama 6
1975 – Notre Dame 13, Alabama 11
2000 – Michigan 35, Aabama 34 (OT)

**The Outback Bowl – Tampa, Florida**
Record: Won 1, Lost 0
1997 – Alabama 17, Michigan 14

**The Rose Bowl – Pasadena, California**
Record: Won 4, Lost 1, Tied 1
1926 – Alabama 20, Washington 19
1927 – Alabama 7, Stanford 7
1931 – Alabama 24, Washington State 0
1935 – Alabama 29, Stanford 13
1938 – California 13, Alabama 0
1946 – Alabama 34, Southern Cal 14

**The Sugar Bowl – New Orleans, Louisiana**
Record: Won 8, Lost 4
1945 – Duke 29, Alabama 26
1948 – Texas 27, Alabama 7
1962 – Alabama 10, Arkansas 3
1964 – Alabama 12, Mississippi 7
1967 – Alabama 34, Nebraska 7
1973 – Notre Dame 24, Alabama 23
1975 – Alabama 13, Penn State 6
1978 – Alabama 35, Ohio State 6
1979 – Alabama 14, Penn State 7
1980 – Alabama 24, Arkansas 9
1990 – Miami (FL) 33, Alabama 25
1993 – Alabama 34, Miami (FL) 13

**The Sun Bowl – El Paso, Texas**
Record: Won 3, Lost 0
1983 – Alabama 28, SMU 7
1986 – Alabama 28, Washington 6
1988 – Alabama 29, Army 28

**Composite Bowl Record:**
Won 30, Lost 21, tied 3

# INDEX

Abbott, Eli, 14, *14*, 110
Alexander, Shaun, 8, 59, 70, 86, *87*, 88, *88*, 92, 110, 123
All-America players, 14, 15, 20, 26, 35, 42, 51, 88, 130
Aloha Bowl, 70, 98
Anderson, Mark, 108, *108*
Angelich, Jim, 35, *35*, 37
Army, 15, 73, 134
Auburn University, 6, *7*, 14, 42, 44, 47, 54, 58, 63, 70, 73, 78, 81, 91, 98, 110, 112, 119, 120, 123

Bailey, David, 123
Bankhead, William, *10*
Barker, Jay, 78, *78*, *79*, 81, *81*, 82, *83*, 84, 91
Barnes, Emil, 27, *27*
Bates, Todd, *96*, 97
Battle, Bill, 120
Battle, Marco, 136
Bay, Bill, 17
Beard, Santonio, 88, *89*, 122, *122*, 123
Beasley, Terry, 110
Beaumont, Eugene, 10, 12, *13*
Bell, Al, 70
Bendross, Jesse, 63
Bennett, Cornelius, 8, *68*, 69, 70, 73
Bennett, Kyle, 107, *107*
Bernier, Charles, 17
Birmingham Athletic Club, 14
Blackburn, Darrell, 82, *82*
Blockbuster Bowl, 75
Blockbuster II Bowl, 83
Bostic, James, 123
Bostick, Brian, 101
Boston College, 38
Bowl Championship Series, 124
Brian Piccolo Award, 75
Brigham Young University, 88
Brooker, Tommy, 120
Brown, Curtis, 81, *81*, 84
Brown, Johnny Mack, 8, 20, 22, *22*, 25, *25*, 27, 28, *28*, 130
Brown, Keith, 104, 106, *106*, 136
Brown, Red, 22
Brown, William, 28, *28*
Bryant, Paul "Bear," 6, 7, 8, *9*, 20, 35, *35*, 36, 37, 39, 48-63, 77, 86, 101, 116, 119, 123, 124, 130, 135
Bryant-Denny Stadium (Tuscaloosa), 6, 20, *62*, 63, 65, 101, 123

Buckler, Bill, 22, 27
Cain, John (Sugar), 8, 26, *26*, 27, 32, *32*
Caldwell, Herschel, 22
Camp, Walter, 10
Campbell, "Monk," 26, *26*, 28, *29*
Carter, Antonio, 91
Case College, 17
Castille, Jeremiah, 136
Castille, Tim, 104
Chicago Bears, 101
Christensen, Jamie, 104, 107, *107*
Citrus Bowl, 78, 81, 82, 136, 139
Clausen, Casey, 101, 103
Clemens, Al, 17
Clements, Tom, 133
Clemson University, 8, 20
Coaches
  Abbott, Eli, 14, *14*
  Beaumont, Eugene, 10, 12, *13*
  Bryant, Paul "Bear," 6, 7, 8, *9*, 48-63, 77
  Curry, Bill, 73, 74
  Drew, Harold (Red), 40-47
  DuBose, Mike, 86-97
  Franchione, Dennis, 92, 95, 96, 97
  Perkins, Ray, 64-72
  Price, Mike, 98
  Saban, Nick, 6, *7*, 107, 108, *108*
  Shula, Mike, 98-108
  Stallings, Gene, 6, *7*, 74-85
  Thomas, Frank, 8, *8*, 30-39, 77
  Wade, Wallace, 8, *8*, 20-29
  Whitworth, J.B., 47
College Football Hall of Fame, 6, 20, 22, 35
Conway, Bob, *128*, 129
Cotton Bowl, 38, 47, 104, 107, 108, 129, 136, 139
Cribbs, Joe, 110
Crisp, Hank, 17, 18, *19*
Croyle, Brodie, 91, 98, *98*, 102, *102*, 103, 104, 136, 139, *139*
Curry, Bill, 69, 73, 74, 81

Dallas Cowboys, 74
Daniels, Tom, 110, 112
Darby, Ken, 104, *104*, *105*
Davis, Terry, 59, *59*
Davis, Tim, 131, *131*
Davis, Wayne, 70
Demyanovich, Joe, 35, *35*, 37
Denny, Dr. George (Mike), 8, 20, 30
Dixon, Gerald, 96
"Dothan Antelope." See Brown, Johnny Mack
Doyle, Phil, 81

Drew, Harold (Red), 40-47, 123
DuBose, Mike, 86-97
Duke, Bobby, 44, *44*
Duke University, 22, 30, 38, 127
Dunham, J.C., 110
Dyess, Martin, 119

Fiesta Bowl, 81, 137
Fracchia, Mike, 51, *51*
Franchione, Dennis, 92, *92*, 95, 96, 97, 123
Francis, Kavanaugh, 35, *35*
Frederickson, Tucker, 110
Fullbacks, 27, 37, 44, 47, 104
Fullmer, Phil, 96

Galloway, Ahmad, 95, *95*
Galloway, Andrew, 123
Georgia Tech, 27, 44, 69, 73
Gillis, Grant, 130
Gilmer, Harry, 8, 35, 38, *38*, *39*, 42, 91, 127, *127*, 133
Grayson, D.A., 14
Grayson, Dave, 112
Green Bay Packers, 36, 42, 47, 73
Guman, Mike, 133

Halfbacks, 37, 47
Hall, D.J., 104, 106, *106*
Hall of Fame Bowl, 73
Hamilton, Tom, 51
Hannah, John, 8
Harmon, Mary, 48
Harper, Roman, *96*, 97
Helms Athletic Foundation, 27
Hill, Murry, 73
Hobson, Clell, 42, *43*
Hodges, Norwood, *126*, 127
Hollingsworth, Gary, 119, *119*
Hood, Chris, *84*, 85
Howard, Frank, 8, 20, 27
Howell, Millard (Dixie), 8, 32, *32*, 35, *35*, 36, 37, 48, 51, 130
Hoying, Bobby, 82, *82*
Hubert, Pooley, 8, 17, 18, *18*, 20, 27, 130
Hudson, Ray, 104
Humphrey, Bobby, 8, 59, 70, *72*, 73
Hunnicut, Lynn, 58, *58*
Hunter, Scott, 54, 123
Hurlbut, Jack, 55
Hutson, Don, 7, 8, 35, *35*, 36, *36*, 37, 48, 51, 130

Independence Bowl, 95, 139
Ingram, Hootie, 8, 78

Iowa State, 95
Iron Bowl, 81, 86, 110, 122, 123
Ivy, Hyrle, 44, *44*

Jackson, Bo, 110
Jackson, Kevin, 85, *85*
Jackson, Quincy, 88
Jackson, Wilbur, 59
James, Chris, *96*, 97
Jenkins, Bobby, 38, *39*
Johnson, Tommy, 84
Jones, Bruce, 27
Jones, Terry, 139, *139*
Jordan, Leroy, 8, 120
Jordan, Shug, 119

Kickers, 8, 17, 36, 42, 47, 63, 70, 104, 120
Kickoff Classic, 69
Kilgrow, Joe, 37, *37*
King, Tyrone, 58, *58*
Krauss, Barry, 133

Lakeview Park (Birmingham), 14
Landry, Tom, 74
Langham, Antonio, 78, 83
Lassic, Derrick, 84
Layne, Bobby, 42
Lee, Bill, 8, 33, *33*, 35, *35*, 37, 48
Legion Field (Birmingham), 20, 65, *112*, 113, 116, 123
Lewis, Tommy, 42, *42*, *43*, 44, *44*, *46*, 47, 129, *129*, 139
Lewis, Walter, 63, 65, *65*, 66, *66*, 69, 91
Liberty Bowl, 52, 54, 63, 135
Linebackers, 8, 15, 20, 26, 27, 35, 37, 69, 70, 73, 101, 120, 133
Little, William G. (W.G.), 10, 11, *11*, 14, 110
Lombardi, Vince, 47
London, Antonio, 81
Louisiana State, 63, 73, 75, 81, 88, 107, 133
Luna, Bobby, 42, *43*, 44, *44*, *45*, 47

Malcolm, Charles, 44, *44*
Malone, Toderick, *74*, 75, 78
Mancha, Vaughan, 8
Mangum, John, 8
Marlow, Bobby, 8, 42, *42*, *43*, 44, 47, 110, 116
Marr, Charlie, 35, *35*
McBride, John, 44, *44*
McElroy, Alan, 63
Miami Dolphins, 101, 107, 108
Michigan State, 59, 107, 133

Miller, Matt, 107, *107*
Milons, Freddie, 8, 88, 91, *91*, 92, *92*, 95, *95*
Mississippi State, 17, 63, 78, 88, 92
Moegle, Dick, 47, 129, *129*, 139
Moore, Ricky, 69
Morrow, Bob, 35, *35*
Music City Bowl, 104
Musso, Johnny, 8, 44, 59, 115, *115*, 123

Namath, Joe, 8, 52, 52, 54, *54*, 55, 58, 91, 110, *114*, 115, 120, 129, *129*, *130*, 131, 136
Nathan, Tony, 110
National Football League (NFL), 7, 36, 42, 47, 55, 64, 73, 74, 77, 86, 88, 98, 101, 107
Naval Academy, 51
Neely, Jess, 139
Neighbors, Billy, 8
Newsome, Ozzie, 8, 58, *58*, 92
New York Giants, 64
New York Jets, 55
Nix, Patrick, 81, *81*
Nobis, Tommy, 136
Notre Dame University, 31, 35, 58, 59, 70

Ogden, Ray, 58, 120
Ogilvie, Major, 63, 133
Ohio State, 63, 69, 78, 81, 82, 136, 139
Oklahoma State, 47
Orange Bowl, 38, 40, 42, 47, 54, 55, 58, 91, 129, 131, 133, 136
Outback Bowl, 84, 85

Palmer, David, 75, *75*, 81, 83
Paterno, Joe, 63
Payne, Greg, 136
Penn State, 54, 59, 69, 70, 116, 133, 135
Perkins, Ray, 8, *9*, 64-72, 81, 86, 98, *114*, 115, 120, 133
Pettus, Gordon, *112*, 113
Phoenix Cardinals, 77
Pollard, J.W.H. (Doc), 14
Pope, Derrick, *96*, 97, 101
Pratt, Derrill, 14
Price, Mike, 98
Probst, Shorty, 17, 18, *18*
Proctor, Michael, 8
Pro Football Hall of Fame, 7
Prothro, Tyrone, 103, 104

Quarterbacks, 8, 20, 36, 37, 42, 47, 54, 55, 58, 59, 60, 65, 66, 67, 78, 81, 82, 91, 98, 103, 113, 114, 115, 116, 120, 123, 133

Reagan, Ronald, 18, *19*
Red Elephant mascot, 6, *6*, 65, *65*
Rice, Bill, 51, *51*
Rice University, 47, 129, 139
Richardson, Jess, 42, *42*
Rockne, Knute, 20, 35, 36
Rose Bowl, 20, 22, 25, 26, 27, 28, 30, 33, 35, 36, 37, 38, 124, 127, 129, 130
Ross, J.P., 14
Running backs, 8, 14, 15, 17, 22, 25, 35, 36, 38, 42, 44, 59, 63, 86, 123, 130
Rupp, Adolph, 52
Rutledge, Gary, 59
Rutledge, Jeff, 59, *59*, 123
Ryans, Demeco, 101, 108, *108*

Saban, Nick, 6, *7*, 107, 108, *108*
St. Lous Football Cardinals, 77
St. Mary's University, 32
Salem, Ed, 8, *112*, 113, 116
Sanders, Red, 51
Sanders, Terry, 63
Savage, Frank, 110
Scott, Xen, 17, 18, *18*
Sewell, Joe, 15, *15*, 17
Sewell, Luke, 17
Shade, Sam, 121, *121*
Shaw, Cliff, 139
Shealy, Steadman, 60, *61*, 63, 115, *115*, 123, 133
Shelton, Bobby, 119
Shula, David, 67, *67*, 70
Shula, Don, 101
Shula, Mike, 8, 98-108, 139, 139
Sington, Fred, 8, 20, 26, *26*, 27
Skelton, Bobby, 51, 54
Sloan, Steve, 8, 54, *54*, 55, 58, 133
Smith, David, 134, *135*, 136
Smith, D.H., 110
Smith, Riley, 8, 35, *35*, 36, *36*, 37
Southern Methodist University, 69
Stabler, Ken, 8, 54, 55, *55*, 110, 120
Stacy, Siran, 81
Stagg, Amos Alonzo, 35, 63, 116
Stallings, Gene, 6, 7, 74-85, 86, 101, 123, 133, 135, 137, *137*, *138*, 139
Stanford University, 22, 25, 27, 33, 36, 38
Starr, Bart, 42, *42*, 47
Staten, Ralph, 82, *82*
Stephenson, Riggs, 15, *15*, 17
Stone, William, 44, *44*
Sugar Bowl, 38, 42, 52, 54, 55, 59, 63, 76, 78, 84, 124, 127, 131, *132*, 133, *133*, 134, 136, 137

Sullivan, Pat, 110
Sun Bowl, 69, 70, 73, 98, 136
Syracuse University, 40, 42, 47

Tackles, 22, 27, 33, 38
Tampa Bay Buccaneers, 73, 86, 98, 101
Teague, George, 76, *76*, 84, 134, 135
Texas A&M, 38, 48, 52, 54, 73, 74, 96, 136
Texas Christian University, 96
Texas Tech, 104, 108, 136
Tharp, Corky, 44, 47
Thomas, Derrick, 8, 73, *73*
Thomas, Frank, 8, *8*, 30-39, 48, 51, 77, 129
Tiffin, Van, 8, 68, *68*, 70, 116, *117*, 123
Todd, Richard, 59
Townsend, Deshea, 8
Trammell, Pat, 8, 54, 110, 113, *113*, 119, 120
Tulane University, 54
Turner, Rory, 70

University of Alabama
  beginnings, 10-19
  Bryant years, 48-63
  DuBose era, 86-97
  Franchione at, 92, 95, 96
  national championships, 6, 8, 9, 20, 22, 25, 26, 27, 28, 30, 33, 35, 36, 37, 38, 48, 52, 54, 58, 59, 60, 63, 69, 76, 77, 78, 83, 115, 133, 135
  NCAA sanctions against, 78, 95, 96, 101
  Perkins years, 64-72
  Saban years, 107-09
  Shula era, 98-108
  Southeastern Conference titles, 6, 27, 35, 37, 52, 59, 66, 83, 86, 119, 123, 124
  Stallings tenure at, 74-85
  Thomas era, 30-39
  "Thomas's War Babies," 38, 42
  unbeaten seasons, 20, 22, 25, 27, 35, 38, 52, 135
  Wade era, 20-29
University of Colorado, 75, 81
University of Florida, 44, 86, 91, 92
University of Georgia, 17, 35, 58, 70
University of Hawaii, 103
University of Illinois, 135
University of Kentucky, 48, 52, 73
University of Maryland, 48, 52
University of Miami, 76, 78, 84, 134, 135
University of Michigan, 73, 85, 91
University of Minnesota, 104

University of Mississippi, 70, 92, 104
University of Nebraska, 58, 59, 133
University of Oklahoma, 55, 101, 136
University of Pennsylvania, 10, 12, 17, 18
University of South Carolina, 92
University of Southern California, 38, 59, 70
University of Southern Mississippi, 83
University of Tennessee, 63, 69, 70, 78, 81, 83, 96, 101, 103, 104
University of Texas, 42
University of Washington, 25, 27, 124, 129

Vanderbilt University, 36, 51
Vandergraaff, W.T. (Bully), 14, 15, *15*, 17
Vaughn, Michael, 88
Virginia Tech, 44

Wade, Wallace, 8, *8*, 20-29, 30, 129, 130
Wahtley, Jim, 35, *35*
Warner, Glenn (Pop), 25, 27, 35, 63
Washington State, 20, 28, 130
Watts, Tyler, 97, *97*
Weber, Robin, 133
Welch, Clem, *112*, 113
Whitman, Steve, 133
Whitmire, Don, 8, 38
Whitworth, J.B., 40, 47
Wide receivers, 8, 78, 104, 114
Williams, Shaud, *100*, 101, 103, *103*
Williams, Sherman, 8, 82, *83*, 136, *138*, 139
Williamson, Richard, 55
Wilson, Delma, 112
Winslett, Hoyt, 22, *24*, 25, *25*
World War II, 7, 8, 38, 51

Zow, Andrew, 88, *90*, 91, *91*, 92, 123

## Photo Credits

Neil Brake: 6, 7 (right), 75 (right), 112 (right), 118, 119 (right), 137 (both)
Chance Brockway: 59-61, 65 (bottom left), 67-68
Brockway & Emmons: 64, 65 (top), 69, 72, 119 (left)
Malcolm Emmons: 111, 116 (both)
Getty Images: 87, 106 (both), 107 (both)
Joseph McNally: 1
Paul W. Bryant Museum/University of Alabama: 7 (left), 12, 15 (left), 19, 25 (both), 28 (left), 40, 42 (both), 44 (left), 45, 73-74, 75 (left), 76-86, 88-105, 108 (both), 109, 114, 115 (left), 117, 120-123, 129 (right), 132-136, 138-139
Bruce Schwartzman: 2, 3, 65 (bottom right), 70
University of Alabama: 8 (left)
University of Alabama, W. S. Hoole Special Collections Library: 10-11, 13-14, 15 (right), 16-17, 18 (left), 112 (left)
UPI/Bettmann Newsphotos: 4, 5, 8 (right), 9 (both), 21, 22 (both), 23-24, 26 (all three), 27, 29-39, 41, 43, 44 (right), 46-58, 62-63, 66, 71, 115 (right), 125-128, 129 (left), 130-131